THE 2-WEEK VACATION TEST

Stop Working "In" Your Business.
Start Living Your Dream Life.

THE ●2-WEEK VACATION TEST

How To Build A Wildly Successful
Business That Can Run & Thrive
Without You

AUSTIN NETZLEY

FOUNDER OF **2X**

THE FREE VACATION TEST TOOLKIT

"Ideas are worthless. Execution is everything."

— **MARK CUBAN**

This book is not designed to just give you ideas. It's designed to forever shift how you use your time and grow your business.

So to help, I've put together a collection of the top resources I've mentioned in this book to help you *implement* these strategies and systems right away.

This will help guide you throughout the book, and make sure it's as easy as possible to implement the key actions I share.

This is valued at $497, but it's 100% FREE as part of this book. It's all in one central place for you here: **www.2X.co/tools**

Inside, you'll find templates, systems, swipes, spreadsheets, worksheets, and more to help you get free and grow a much healthier business and team. You can access the FREE toolkit directly here:

>> 2X.CO/TOOLS <<

CONTENTS

INTRODUCTION

> ## *"Hey, wake up. Can you call 911? I feel like I'm dying."*

I was lying on the bed of a crappy hotel, and the paramedics were checking me out.

They checked my pulse. Listened to my heart. Did the full review.

I was answering the medic's questions, telling him a bit about my situation. I told him about my business, the long hours, the late nights. I told him everything and was proud of my work and mission.

And yet I'll never forget. He looked at me with the saddest look I've ever seen.

He was not impressed. In fact, it was clear that he just felt bad for me.

Until this point, I was *hustling*. I was grinding. I was putting in the work—doing what I *thought* I was supposed to do.

I wanted wealth and success so bad. There wasn't anything I wanted more.

So I was building my business, grinding every moment of every day… until my body just gave up.

I was fit as can be, as an ex-college football player running marathons and 10+ mile obstacle-course races for fun. Yet here I was, at 26 years young, having to call 911. I was so stressed out, exhausted, and overwhelmed from my business that I started having anxiety attacks. I couldn't breathe or sleep.

I was delirious lying in bed, but every time I drifted often to sleep, I would stop breathing and pop up in bed, gasping for breath.

I thought for sure I was going to die, but the medics said I was fine. They told me it was an anxiety attack and that I needed to reduce my stress and get more sleep. I did as they said—I got into bed earlier at night and made a few changes, but it didn't last. I didn't fix things at the root, and got back to my typical *hustle* ways shortly after.

And then, in eerily similar fashion, 12 months later, my anxiety attacks returned and I had to call for help again.

The first one spooked me. It opened my eyes and made me aware of the changes I needed to make. Yet, I quickly got consumed again by the grind of business, trying to become successful, putting my health on the line. I thought I could power through it.

But that second time—that's when things shifted. That was proof I *had* to change. My life depended on it.

Exhausted, overwhelmed, and struggling to grow, I knew in my heart of hearts:

> ## *"There __has__ to be a better, simpler way to scale a successful business."*

I knew others were succeeding *without* having to work 80-hour work weeks back-to-back-to-back. Or ever. I knew entrepreneurship shouldn't require a Herculean effort, especially not for this long.

I wanted to make a big impact, build a thriving multi-million-dollar business, yet *not* have to work crazy hours or be stressed all the time. So figuring out how to have big success in business while *also* having time freedom was my new mission—and my fire burned as bright as ever to figure it out.

So, I took a mini-retirement to travel the world and recharge after my first business... And then committed the last 8+ years to master the game of business success *without* the grind.

But I wish I could tell you it was all sunshine and rainbows from there. Unfortunately, it was not.

As I was finishing my travels, I started a passion project that quickly led to building my first agency. With the agency, we got traction immediately, generating over $500,000 in revenue quickly—but then we stalled out and it started to become a *grind* to grow.

Even with a small team of really solid people, I found myself stuck in a similar position again. I was overworked, overwhelmed, and underpaid. I was working long hours each week, and with a rollercoaster of emotions—one moment things were good, the next would be full of stress and fires. I felt responsible for nearly every part of my business, and it started to become more and more frustrating.

Every month, we'd be working hard—but we weren't really getting ahead. We were officially on the hamster-wheel going nowhere fast, and I was stuck in the middle of it.

After nearly a year of this and on the path to burnout again, I was fed up. I wasn't going back to the anxiety attacks. I was ready for my success to feel *easier* for once. I was ready for my vision of achieving a seven-figure business while also having time freedom to be a reality. I still believed it was possible.

So, in lust in a new relationship and frustrated with my business, I did something crazy...

Even though my business was far from ready to operate without me, I decided to take my girlfriend (who was a teacher) and go travel all summer. She had summers off, and her break started in only six weeks time. So, on a whim, we planned over two months of travel, and made it happen.

At first, this was for me. I needed to recharge, reduce my stress, and get perspective on what to do with the business to scale it to the next level.

But then I quickly realized...

This is the best thing I can do for:

- My team
- Our operations
- My mindset and letting go...

And ultimately, the long-term growth and success of my company.

I realized that the path to what I wanted was accelerated dramatically through taking time off.

It forced me to pull myself out of the day-to-day grind, stopping trying to do everything myself.

It helped me improve my operations and team, getting them to thrive without me.

It helped me simplify my business to the core, seeing exactly who we were best to serve and how we were going to scale by focusing on *less*.

It helped me identify and fix our key gaps and issues head-on, and we made more progress in a few weeks than we had in many months.

That summer of travel turned out to be the best business move I could have made. It helped me start *living* and running my business—no longer being *owned* by my business.

It was eye opening, life-changing, and a complete up-leveling of my business and lifestyle. And it happened fast.

So this immediately changed my perspective and approach to business—and helped create the exact process I'm going to teach you in this book.

Since that time, I went on to scale numerous seven-figure businesses in the next few years, hitting the Inc. 5000 fastest-growing companies in the U.S. in back-to-back years while also having a ton of time freedom.

One of those businesses is my coaching company, 2X, which helps ambitious entrepreneurs implement the systems and strategies to scale consistently *without* the chaos and overwhelm. And after years helping guide over 1,000 six- and seven-figure entrepreneurs to *way* more growth and success, I can assure you:

You truly can have big success *and* time freedom. A thriving business *and* an incredible lifestyle.

And in fact, business success and time freedom both go hand in hand.

The way we see it at my coaching company 2X is, there are three key signs of a wildly successful business:

1. You're **scaling** with consistency and control
2. You're generating **strong profits** and cash flow (and ultimately wealth!)
3. And you have **time freedom**—you are not stuck "in" the business, overwhelmed or overworked...

So you can live what we call your "Level 10 Life." This means being balanced, having fun, putting family first, and creating experiences to live what you define as an amazing life—*while* also being wildly successful. This is not about an "OK" or "good" life, it's about a 10 out of 10—your dream life.

It's super easy to get one of these three from your business. It's pretty easy to get two. But it's extremely hard to get all three.

Well, this book contains the proven unique process we've optimized for years to help you get all three. I'm going to show you how to achieve growth, wealth, *and* freedom.

And I've learned over the years, it's that last one—time freedom—that is actually the catalyst of it all. This is the driver that will lead to the success you dream of.

The bad news is, time freedom is a top issue for entrepreneurs. In fact:

Studies show that most entrepreneurs work *more* and earn less than they would in a job.[1]

One crazy stat from The New York Enterprise Report[2] showed that **small-business owners work twice as much as regular employees.**

You became an entrepreneur because you want to work twice as much? I don't think so.

The bad thing is, the crazy work hours become *normal.* You get sucked in. *"You have to do what you have to do,"* as we tell ourselves… and next thing you know, years go by with you hustling and grinding—but with little to show for it.

And not only do you sacrifice, but your kids, family, friends, health and relationships have to suffer as well. That is not acceptable.

You are reading this because you know that you're capable of so much more. I knew I was too. That's why I created my coaching company and wrote this book: to show you a better, simpler way to scale that we learned through years of experience and over 1,000 businesses. Our mission is to help you take back control of your time, and create the business success and Level 10 Life you know is possible.

Business is just part of a great life.

I mean, what is all the work for if you can't enjoy your life?

You don't get in the car until you know where you're going, yet so many entrepreneurs are hustling hard but forget what they're even trying to achieve! So the first step in this process is to get recentered on what that dream vision is for you.

> What is your Level 10 Life? What are you trying to achieve? What does your dream business look like? How are you ideally spending your time? With whom? How much are you earning? And what does your life look like *outside* of business?

Get clear on this, as your vision drives everything. That is the destination, and that is what we'll help you achieve with this book.

The way that we're going to get there as fast and easily as possible? It's all summarized down into a unique process to build up towards:

> A two-week, no-strings-attached vacation
> away from your business.

This counterintuitive approach can change everything.

Imagine if, right now, you took off on a two-week no-strings-attached vacation away from your business...

Where you are 100 percent off the grid, fully disconnected, with no:

- Internet
- Laptop
- Phone
- Connection to your email or team

What would happen to your business?

What would happen to your income? Your team and operations? Your clients and customers?

And most importantly, *how would you feel?*

Would you be on the beach, toes in the sand, without a care in the world? Or would your little vacation morph into two weeks of stress as you *try* to enjoy family time but can't stop worrying about all that you *aren't* doing for your business?

Most business owners would have to admit it looks more like the latter.

Well, I'm here to tell you: that is not OK! That is not why you started your business. That is not what success is.

As an ambitious entrepreneur, business success is a key part of your dream life. That's OK. What's *not* OK is when we get so consumed by our businesses that we lose track of what's really important.

But the fact is:

If you can't take two weeks off from your business, you don't have a business. You have a self-employed job.

You have a trap that you've created for yourself, creating more work and stress with less of what you really want.

I've been there. And unfortunately, this is the reality for the vast majority of entrepreneurs—whether they realize it or not.

We have to fix this, and we will—one strategic step at a time.

The solution is to get your business ready for a two-week vacation where you are fully disconnected from your business. This "test" will show you the *true* health of your company.

Now, as you go on that extended break fully separated from your team, operations, and clients, one of four outcomes will happen. We break these down into four stages:

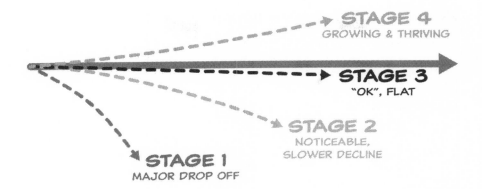

- **Stage 1**: Your business fails quickly without you operating it.
- **Stage 2**: Your business slowly fails and starts to fall apart without your direction and work.
- **Stage 3**: Things are able to operate fine without you temporarily, but the business does not advance while you're out.
- **Stage 4**: Your business still thrives and grows without you! This is where you want to be.

A way we can simplify this down is this:

Stage 1: You *are* the business.

Stage 2: Stuck "in" the business.

Stage 3: Working "on" the business.

Stage 4: Flying *above* the business.

For many reasons, the vast majority of small-business owners get stuck in Stage 2 (working "in" the business) and can never break free.

With The 2-Week Vacation Test™, you escape the day-to-day operations intentionally and jump straight to Stage 4—getting fully detached from your business temporarily.

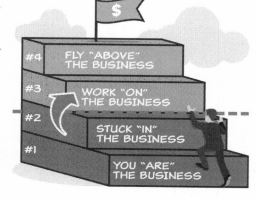

This helps you officially break the strong ties of being *owned* by your business and helps you improve your team and operations. Then from here, you have the opportunity to make it permanent and work in Stages 3 and 4 ongoing (and officially staying out of Stages 1 and 2).

This is working strategically "on" your business—while having complete control of your time. Not only does this benefit your lifestyle, it also leads to a much stronger business that is ready to scale.

This book is all about getting you to Stage 4—where things can run, thrive, and grow *without* you!

Once you're a Stage 4 business:

- Your team and operations are set and thriving (without you)
- You can work as much or little as you want (and on the things you enjoy)
- Your team has more autonomy and ownership, leading to more satisfaction and growth

- You are recharged and energized, in control of your time
- You can see your business so much more clearly and strategically, knowing exactly what you need to do to improve
- You are exponentially more likely to scale, as your business is no longer dependent on your hours

Once you're here, you can achieve the business success *and* life you dream of!

Plus, you then have *optionality*. Do you want to scale faster? Work less while you still produce strong profits? Exit for a high valuation? You get to choose because you have a much healthier and more scalable business along with the time freedom of where you want to focus.

Long story short, the path to everything you want to achieve in business is through The 2-Week Vacation Test™.

Once you get to Stage 4, you will be in the elite club of entrepreneurs. And the cool thing is, you aren't as far away from this as you may think.

We have had so many private coaching clients go from being owned by their business to completely shifting their time and lifestyle forever in just a few short weeks—while also scaling fast to the next level.

By following the suggestions I've outlined in this book, they've created growing businesses that can run and thrive *without* so much dependency on them in countless industries and niches across the globe.

Our 2X client Erin hadn't taken a *weekend* off in 20 years, never mind a whole week. Seriously, no weekends off in 20 years! After a few of these shifts, she started taking every weekend off, and has enjoyed three *entire* weeks off in her first four months since implementing some of these strategies.

Another client, Liz, just got back from a 12-day trip to Dubai and only spent one hour on work. She now has plans to do these big trips very regularly, even with her business and team growing faster than ever.

Within two months, Kyle and his wife Christie took a trip to Hawaii where Kyle was actually present on vacation for *"the first time in forever,"* according to Christie. Oh, and they made $170,000 in those two weeks (which is up dramatically from $88,000 per month before joining 2X).

So how did they do it? And how can *you* get your business 'vacation ready'?

We are going to break that down step-by-step through a proven process that will start separating you from the attachment of your business right away.

THE FREEDOM RAMP-UP PROCESS

"The secret of getting ahead is getting started. The secret of getting started is breaking your complex overwhelming tasks into small manageable tasks, and starting on the first one."
— **MARK TWAIN**

Imagine yourself coming back from a two-week, no-strings-attached vacation with your family.

You didn't work at all. You slept like a baby, laughed, played, and were fully recharged.

And you knew with confidence the entire time, your business was thriving just fine without you.

You have an elite team, you're working reasonable hours (on mostly all things you enjoy), always stopping work on time to be with family, are no longer stressed out constantly, and you're in complete control of your time.

At the center of your life is now *your life – not* your business.

You're still passionate and driven—in fact, more than ever.

You're still growing fast and making big business moves—again, more than ever.

But now it is all done with *intentionality*. Now, you're in control. **Now you own your business, not the other way around.**

You look around and see: you are truly living your dream life.

Finally!

Just picture this moment. Feel into it.

It feels good, right?

Well, let's make that a reality and as quickly as possible.

The way that we're going to do that is to build up towards the two-week break, one strategic step at a time with what we call The Freedom Ramp-Up Process.

This is a series of six key milestones that will help you make progress through much easier steps, building up towards your ultimate test—the two-week no-strings-attached vacation.

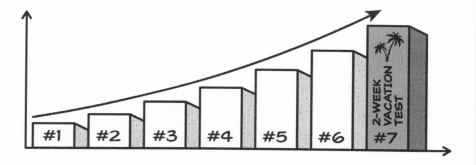

Each milestone will stack on top of each other, and there will be specific systems and strategies to succeed for each one.

The six milestones are:

1. One Evening 100% Off
2. One Weekend 100% Off
3. Done By 10:30AM™
4. Full "Crush It" Day
5. Mini-Vacation
6. One Week 100% Off
7. The 2-Week Vacation Test™

With this ramp-up approach:

- You start to detach yourself from your business starting immediately
- You quickly reduce your overwhelm and the amount of tasks you manage
- You build your trust and confidence in your team over time (with small steps)
- They build confidence in *themselves* (and have more autonomy)
- You improve your operations and execution substantially
- You reduce the risks of being completely off (giving you peace of mind for when you are out)
- You shift your mindset with each step, letting go more and more
- You identify and fix the gaps and core issues along the way
- And you accelerate the progress of your business success through small, manageable actions

Done right, this will make things smooth and easy so that when you get to two full no-strings-attached weeks off, it's a breeze!

Plus, you will build a lot of momentum along the way with wins at each step.

With this approach, we are going to do two things:

1. First, we're going to break your *mental* attachment to your business.
2. Second, we'll get you *physically* detached from the business.

We will break the cycle you've been stuck in, and quickly change how you approach your time and business. This will lead to more progress in the next few weeks than you likely have in many months.

But first, before we get started, you have to do the first task.

No matter if you're ready or not. No matter if you're scared…

No matter if you are so stuck inside your business right now that you couldn't imagine taking even two full days off, let alone two weeks… here's the first task that you must do:

Set the date for your two-week vacation right now – ideally for some time in the next six months.

You need that urgency. You need that push. You need a deadline to get ready for so that you take the actions needed.

Parkinson's Law states that no matter how long you give yourself, you'll take that much time. The time it takes to do something expands to fit how long you give it. The law is real, and it affects everything.

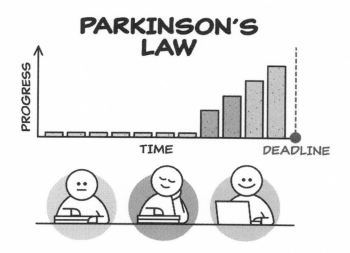

If you don't set a date, it may always get pushed to "someday"—which, as you've experienced, never comes. Or if the date is too far out, you won't get into motion in the short-term. But we want to use some urgency so the necessary shifts occur.

So, set a date that will stretch you and challenge you. One that makes you a bit nervous. One that will require you to _change_ what you've been doing and forever shift your time.

Put it on the calendar. Block it off right now.

Then, fully commit by telling your friends, family, and team. Have them help hold you accountable, as they all win by doing so.

This will be your deadline. This is a critical piece, so don't go on until you do this first step.

As soon as you set that date, your mindset immediately begins to shift. So pick a date, lock it in on the calendar, and let's get you ready to go!

My 2-Week Vacation Date Is: _____

Now that we have that set, let's jump into the first milestone and start getting you some wins.

ONE NIGHT 100% OFF

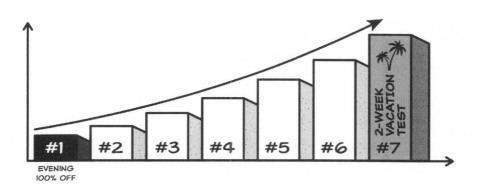

Why did you start your business to begin with?

I'm guessing it was for various forms of *FREEDOM*. Freedom to control your destiny, have more flexibility, make more money, make a bigger impact, and live an incredible lifestyle.

You started your business with such good intentions… But here you are: likely working and stressing way too much.

Even when you're not working, you're still often thinking about work and all that you have to do.

And the thing is, you probably have been dealing with this same issue for a long time. I know because I was there.

We have to change that, and we will, one key step at a time.

The first step is that we have to accept reality.

And part of that reality is this:

You secretly love the chaos. You secretly love the hustle and bustle.

You may not know it, but we often get addicted to our business.

We get addicted to feeling *needed* and smart. We secretly love jumping in and being the hero. Our ego LOVES that.

We secretly crave that dopamine hit we got from the early days of starting and building our businesses:

- Being the do-it-all superhero
- Figuring out how to do *new* things
- Doing a fresh new marketing campaign
- Completing tasks (the easier, the better)

- Having our team or clients feel like we're so special and great at what we do

There's a zest and energy from that. We get pride from it. We feel the all-so-powerful *purpose* from that.

Our lizard brain loves this and gets wired to crave more.

In addition to that, as we build in the first few levels of business success, we learn that more work leads to more revenue. So we're chasing more and more revenue to grow and "be successful" at all costs...

And little by little, without us knowing it, we get consumed by our businesses. Then weeks and weeks go by until it becomes the new normal. We're still addicted, but like any addiction, the fun wears off quickly, leaving only the stress and a business trap with big expenses. Then, you have to keep pushing sales to cover your expenses, and you find yourself on the hamster wheel.

We need to start to break this cycle and create a whole new reality—one that is built with intention.

And here's another thing we need to fix: your inability to *stop* working.

If you're anything like I used to be, you can't fully disconnect. You can't turn it off. You can't stop your mind from working. You can't be fully present.

But your family and friends deserve better. Heck, *you* deserve better.

Let's begin by breaking your mental attachment to your business. From there, you can fully unplug and still have your business and team humming.

So let's start that process, one small step at a time.

The first milestone is simple: **take one weekday evening fully disconnected from your business.**

Don't check anything related to work (including email and social media), or do a single business activity from at least 5PM to 8AM the next day.

You may think this will be easy, but try it tonight. You will likely feel the urge to check things or think about work. Don't!

If you can't easily take a weeknight off from your business, you are addicted to your business.

I have been here many times! I know how hard it can be to leave work behind, even for a night. But you have to break that cycle. Starting tonight.

This is an easy, low-impact first milestone to start to detach and help you see just how addicted you are. So try it. Be fully present with your family, friends, and self.

As you do, be aware of your urges to work, check things, stress, and think about your to-do list and the issues you have to deal with. Write these impulses down as they come up. By doing so, you make them tangible and can more easily address them.

The first step in fixing anything is awareness. So, notice your addiction to the *busyness* of business.

My good friend and one of the best entrepreneurs I know, Chandler Bolt, does this well. He has a very successful eight-figure business, SelfPublishing.com. He works really hard, but the thing is: his hours are in his full control.

When he's working, he's focused and working. When he's not working, he's not working. At all. He doesn't check his team communication tools—in fact, he doesn't even have them on his phone. He rarely checks his email at all (his assistant handles that), let alone during his off hours.

He works hard, but can disconnect and turn it off, even while scaling (fast) and managing a big team and business. And this ability to take a break helps him focus much better when he *is* working, which then leads to way more success. So the point is:

When you're working, work. When you're not, don't. Be able to turn it off.

This first test will help make it happen. It'll help you see: Can you detach? Can you be present? Can you stop the chaos and unplug?

And I get it, it's easier said than done at first. There's a lot of money on the line and there's a lot to do, but more than that, there's an emotional attachment. Your business is your baby. Your success is part of your *identity*.

And you care. In fact, you care so much that you're willing to sacrifice a lot of time you could spend in other ways to work on your business. I get it.

But you have to stop believing that you are your business. You must separate your self-worth from the worth of the business and also realize what I've been talking about: holding on to tasks and working so much is in fact holding you back!

We will get you free, one strategic step at a time—starting with this one night off.

My goal is that this process will be life-changing for you, as it has been for me and many others. So I encourage you: Trust me. Trust this process. And take back control, one step at a time.

You'll feel the impact in various ways right from the start.

THE HEALTH IMPACT

> "Almost everything will work again if you unplug it for a few minutes, including you."
> — **ANNE LAMOTT**

As you complete the one-night-off exercise, you'll likely feel some mental relief. You'll also start to feel the difference in your body and stress levels.

Well, if that's true, that doesn't surprise me in the slightest. The addiction to your business hurts your potential business success and impacts your mental health, but beyond that, it can also lead to poor physical health. Whether you know it or not, your body carries a lot of stress from business and it's a vicious cycle we have to break.

Studies[3] show that entrepreneurs are:

- Twice as likely to have depression compared to typical employees.
- Three times as likely to struggle with an addiction compared to typical employees.

Researchers at the University of Bergen also discovered that workaholism, often seen in entrepreneurs, is associated with an increased risk of psychiatric disorders, including ADHD, OCD, anxiety, and depression.[4]

A study from the World Health Organization[5] found that working an average of 55 hours or more each week increases your risk of stroke by 35 percent and your risk of dying from heart disease by 17 percent, compared to averaging a 35–40-hour workweek.

It's simple: past a certain point, working more hours has a negative impact on your health (whether you realize it or not).

And you may read all this and think, like I did: *"Oh, that's for most people—but not for me. I'm healthy. I'm not at risk of those things."*

But trust me: You are. And it's impacting your health and life more than you may think.

Since your health and success are connected, it's time to start treating yourself like a professional athlete. It's time to take your health, diet, energy, mindset, relationships, and everything more seriously—because it's all connected.

One way of improving your well-being that we can all agree on (and start implementing tonight) is with the cornerstone health habit: sleep.

Your sleep impacts your:

- Mindset
- Energy
- Focus
- Decision making
- Happiness
- Patience
- Leadership
- And much more

With good sleep, you probably feel like a superhero. I know I do. But without it, everything is so much harder, more stressful and less successful.

And it's no surprise, most entrepreneurs struggle with sleep. With the stress, long hours, late nights, and your mind constantly running, many get stuck in this never-ending hamster wheel.

It's a vicious cycle that you must break.

The first major step is simply stopping work. Turn it off. Take one night off, and then slowly move to make your habit of *not* working after-hours permanent.

As you start to implement the steps in this book, you'll realize just how stressed you've been. And you'll notice the positive impact a less-stressed life has on sleep!

THE SLEEP & STRESS CYCLE

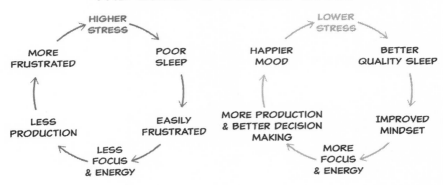

In turn, better sleep = better focus = better business and life.

And it all starts by being able to "turn it off."

So how do you effectively end your workday and set yourself up for success with a more peaceful evening and better sleep? That's what we'll cover next...

THE WRAP-UP ROUTINE

> "The best way to have a good life is to have a good separation between your work life and your personal life."
> — **CAL NEWPORT**

In business, there are two things you can control: how you start your day and how you end your day.

Oftentimes what happens in between can be a blur (at least until we help you improve your time and operations with this book).

But one key system that you can start implementing immediately that will help you work less, be more present, and be much more effective is what we call the Wrap-Up Routine.

This is a simple process to work through at the end of your workday, which will help you:

- Officially end your day and shut off your mind from business
- Reflect, learn, and improve
- Delegate and get things off of your plate
- While also getting the next day set up for success.

This priceless process is easy to do. Simply, at the end of your day, spend 10–15 minutes working through the following process:

1: REFLECT

Spend a few minutes to review the following:

- **Big 3**: Did you get your top three tasks done for the day—especially your #1 thing? If not, why not?

- **Wins:** What were the top wins? Write these down and celebrate your successes.
- **Lessons:** What did you learn? List one to three key lessons from the day. Writing these down makes it more likely the lessons will sink in.
- **Improvements:** Surely, some things happened that could use improvement—systems to create or fix, or opportunities you have yet to act on. List out a couple that come to mind.

2: DO A TIME CHECK

Where did your time and energy go today? Was it focused on the right things or spread in 100 directions? And specifically, what changes related to your time do you need to make to be more effective and less overwhelmed?

You can list out the following:

- **Non-CEO:** What tasks did you spend time on that are low-value activities that you should not be doing as CEO? We'll break this down in more detail in the coming chapters, but list where your time went that you know it really shouldn't be.
- **Energy Drainers:** What took your energy that you can offload?
- **Systems Fixes:** What systems can you create or improve so that you can free up time or drive more results?

Get clear on a couple of time changes to make.

3: PLAN THE NEXT DAY

Then, look over your next few days. See what's on the calendar upcoming, and start to plan ahead.

Then create your specific plan for the next day, listing out your "Big 3"—the top three actions you're committed to complete. By planning in advance, your subconscious mind can work on the solutions for these items overnight, and you can start your next workday ready to dive right in.

> # So many people don't have a plan going into their day, and that has them be reactive right from the start.

Make sure this isn't you.

Now, you'll finalize this plan in the morning before your first work "sprint" which I'll talk about later. But having the first version makes it so much easier to later optimize and go.

4: DELEGATE & COMMUNICATE

Now that you've finished your reflection and time review, and have more clarity of the next few days, it's time to offload things and communicate to your team. This way, they too can plan ahead, help take things off your plate, and create their own success plans.

By further planning ahead, you can reduce reactivity within your team and help everyone get more productive work done. Plus, you offload things while they're fresh in your mind, so you can be more focused the next day.

Every day for the next few weeks (as we go through the process of getting you free), you'll realize that there are some simple things to fix or offload to help free up your time—so do this daily!

And lastly…

5: THE TRIGGER

A great way to end your Wrap-Up Routine is to also have a trigger that signals to your brain it's time to shift gears and go into the rest of your evening.

I like to go for a short walk outside to have a clear break from my computer and working energy. I find this really helps me shift into a more relaxed state for the rest of my night. This way, you don't carry the stress and take your work home with you. You have a clear separation.

My friend Chandler, who I mentioned earlier, uses another hack. Even though he's working from home, he changes out of his "work clothes" into something more relaxed or at least different. This is a mental trigger for him to switch modes.

So create your own trigger, and start using the Wrap-Up Routine immediately. It'll take you 10–15 minutes to do at first. But then after some time, you can wrap up and plan the next day in just a few minutes.

By taking time to reflect and plan, you will have more awareness, be less likely to make the same mistakes, and get better focused on what actions to take. If you do this, you have the opportunity to get better every. Single. Day.

It's powerful.

You can use the template in your Vacation Test Toolkit at 2X.co/tools to help make it easy.

TACTICAL TIP: SCHEDULE FUN

> "Never get so busy making a living that
> you forget to make a life."
> — **DOLLY PARTON**

One of the easiest ways to ensure you separate from work is to have something that is clearly more enjoyable than work planned.

Maybe this is a date night with your spouse, taking your kids on an adventure, a special workout class, or new experience.

Whatever it is, schedule things that fill you up outside of work. And then set them as a ritual so you don't have to think about it.

I personally love to go into a week and know what my plans are for most of my evenings—even if they're planned as a placeholder. That's part of my weekly plan. There is some flexibility with this as new things come up, but this way I'm not going into each evening wondering what I should do (and just end up working too long).

So brainstorm a handful of things that you enjoy more than work that you can do for the evenings. Then plan out a few of these over the coming week, and you'll start to see how much easier it is to separate from work.

If you don't give yourself a clear cut-off and something else to do, we'll find a reason to think about work. But it's time to separate and create your dream *Level 10 Life*—and start living it now!

MILESTONE #1: THE BIG IDEAS

- We often don't realize it, but we get addicted to our business. Our lizard brain loves easy tasks and feeling needed—so we keep doing those things, thus staying on the hamster wheel and "in" the business.

- Before we break the physical attachment to your business and all of the tasks you handle, we first have to break the mental attachment and addiction to your business. Awareness is the first step to making that happen, so notice your tendencies and fix them head on.

- When you're working, work. When you're not, don't. You have to be able to turn work off to live your Level 10 Life.

- Working too much impacts your health, whether you realize it or not. So getting a better grasp on your work time and stress will have a positive impact on your health, which in turn leads to positive impacts on your business.

- Sleep is the cornerstone habit that impacts everything else. With lower stress, more control of your time, and the ability to stop work effectively, you're exponentially more likely to get quality sleep which makes everything easier.

- The Wrap-Up Routine helps you have a clear end to your day that helps you: improve every single day, delegate and offload things daily, be more proactive, and create a plan for the next day so you start your day with momentum. This also helps you clearly end your work day, moving from work mode into your personal life.

- You must have a clear plan going into the day, otherwise, you'll have reactivity right from the start. That starts with the Wrap-Up Routine.
- One of the easiest and best ways to separate yourself from your business is to schedule more fun things outside of business. Play is essential.

WEEKEND
100% OFF

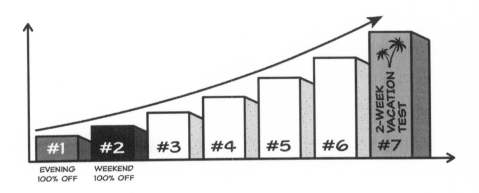

Ah, the weekends. This is supposed to be your time off for fun, recharging, family, friends, and faith.

But are you still working? Or at the least, still stressing about work even when you are off?

Studies show that the majority of entrepreneurs work six or more days each week, while only 7 percent work less than five days.[6]

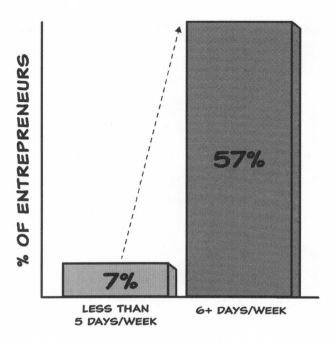

A Bank of America report found that 41 percent of small business owners sacrifice the majority of their free time to manage their business—which so often leaks into the weekends.[7]

It's crazy to think that taking a weekend off is a big deal. You didn't know this when you started in business, but it happens all too often.

Remember Erin, who hadn't taken a weekend off in 20 years? She realized that working weekends wasn't actually helping her business like she thought. In fact, it was doing nothing but keeping her from everything she really wanted! Now she takes every weekend off, and enjoyed three *full* weeks off in her first four months with us. That helped lead her to a much more thriving business and way more time freedom than ever.

It all started with these exact first steps.

And the reality is, if you don't take time off, you'll eventually have to take time off.

If you can't turn it off or recharge, sooner or later, you'll burn out.

I know this from experience. As I shared to start this book, I had anxiety attacks so bad that I couldn't breathe or sleep. Every time I drifted off to sleep, I'd burst up in bed gasping for air. I thought I was going to die, even though I was in my mid-20s and as fit as can be.

It is not worth it to grind past a certain amount. If you tap into your "personal time" to work, you're much more likely to hit a wall.

We've had countless clients come into our 2X coaching program who have dealt with similar stories.

One of our clients, John Murphy, found himself overworked and burnt out. He was working 110 hours per week at the time. He said, *"One morning, it all hit me. I started crying in my cereal, and my wife told me I had to change something."*

Fast-forward a mere four months later, and he was down to 10 hours per week by following our proven 2X system and these steps. He had so much free time that he didn't know what to do with it!

I want to give you that luxury, as well. I want you to have so much free time that you have to figure out new ways to spend it.

Big changes can happen fast…if you follow the process.

So take back control. Shut your laptop and work applications—including email, team communication, and social media. And do zero work from the close of Friday until Monday morning.

I bet you'll feel more mentally refreshed and back in control, ready for a productive week—but don't take my word for it. Try it, and see for yourself.

To do this, we need to take back control of your time and free up capacity. So in this chapter, we're going to talk about:

1. Understanding what true productivity is (and isn't)
2. Getting clear on the true value of your time
3. How to free up time and start doing much less immediately
4. And adding a bookend to your week to set yourself up for success

Let's get started.

THE MYTHS OF PRODUCTIVITY

"Being busy is not the same as being productive.
In fact, being busy is a form of laziness—lazy
thinking and indiscriminate action."
— **TIM FERRISS**

When you think about productivity, you likely think it's about getting more things done.

You're looking for tools and tactics to be able to do more.

But there's a lot of problems with this thinking.

The key is that it's still reliant on one thing: YOU.

Real productivity isn't this. Real productivity is defined as "the effectiveness of productive effort, as measured in terms of the rate of output per unit of input."[8]

Put more simply it's this:

$$\textbf{PRODUCTIVITY} = \frac{\textbf{OUTPUT}}{\textbf{INPUT}}$$

It's about increasing your output compared to your input.

Productivity is about working *smarter*, not harder.

Secondly, in business, you have a special option available to you:

Real productivity isn't simply about *your* output. It's about your team's overall output.

Even if you have people who can do something 70 percent as good as you, if you have three of them doing a particular function for you, they can achieve 210 percent of what you can—while you work zero on that thing.

That is *real* productivity (increasing the overall output while decreasing your personal input). That's *leverage*. The wealthy and most successful entrepreneurs love leverage, and you should too!

The other myth about productivity is related to your hours. We can get so caught up in the blur of business and all that we have to do that we overwork.

A study featured in Harvard Business Review[9] found that 60 percent of those who carry smartphones for work are connected to their jobs 13.5 or more hours a day on weekdays and about five hours on weekends. **That's a total of about 72 hours per week!**

But here's the thing:

Studies showed that humans can only focus fully for up to four to five hours a day.[9] That means, we only have, at most, four to five hours per day of truly productive work. And for most, it's much less with the chaos and reactivity of a small business.

Again:

More hours doesn't not mean more productivity.

In fact, there was a super interesting study that proved this.

Stanford University economist John Pencavel found that **productivity drops significantly after a 50-hour work week.**[10]

And further:

Productivity plummets after 55 hours to the point that someone who puts in 70 hours doesn't produce anything more with those extra 15 hours!

Sure, every once in a while, you may have a time that requires extra work to get a big project done. But grinding week-in and week-out is actually *hurting* your productivity.

Here's another way to look at it. **Over time, the grinding weeks wear you down. Focus, energy, motivation, and morale all decline. And as a result, your productivity gets worse.**

Whereas consistently being balanced and focused wins over time.

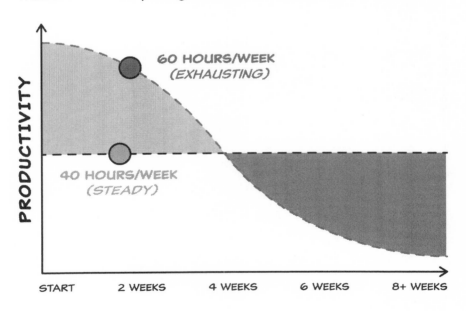

So what you'll learn over time is that working too much is the *exact thing* that is keeping you from what you really want, and the success you know is possible.

Work smarter, not harder.

> ## Business is a marathon, not a sprint. Play the long game by working smarter – which means working *less* with more intentionality.

Shift your mindset.

This means working strategically—not hustling and grinding. Intentionality is how you get ahead long term.

And the second milestone is helping you do just that. Take the weekend 100 percent off. It'll lead to a lot of good overall.

To get you comfortable with taking more time off, we need to reduce the overwhelm, reduce the decision fatigue, and free up capacity.

To help do that, we need to know…

"You don't get paid for the hour. You get paid for the value you bring to the hour."

— **JIM ROHN**

Not all time is created equal. In fact, it's wildly disproportionate.

To make big changes to your business, revenue and wealth, we have to level up the value of your time. But do you know yours? And are you making decisions based on that? Let's figure that out now.

Simply divide the total earnings you want to make in the year ahead by the hours worked to get your hourly rate. Use this calculation:

$$\frac{\text{Target Earnings}}{\text{Hours Per Week} \times \text{Weeks Worked Per Year}} = \text{Average Value of Time (\$/Hour)}$$

Let's say you want to take home $400,000 in personal earnings this year (total of salary and distributions). And for simplicity's sake, divide that by 2,000 (which assumes you work on average 40 hours per week and 50 weeks per year). So, this would mean that your earnings need to average $200 per hour.

So for every hour you spend doing $10 per hour admin activities, you need to replace that with a $400-per-hour activity to get to your average.

Or put another way...

> # Every hour you spend on $10 per hour admin tasks, you are literally losing $190!

So think of that next time you're working on something admin-related. **You are paying $190 to work on something that you probably don't even enjoy!**

Plus, you can find someone who not only enjoys that work a lot more— they are likely *much better* at it than you are.

That is painful.

By knowing the value of your time, you make better decisions about what you need to let go of and stop trying to be a jack-of-all-trades superhero. That's not a smart way to scale.

The key thing is to offload as much at the bottom end low-value tasks, and increase your high-impact activities. One way we think about it is with *The 2X Delegation Rule.*

> # The 2X Delegation Rule: you should delegate anything and everything that is less than half of your hourly rate.

So if your rate needs to be $200 per hour (per the above example), then you should work to offload anything and everything that you can hire out for under $100 per hour. And do you know how much you can offload and delegate for under $100 per hour? Pretty much anything!

Let's make this tangible.

THE TIME TABLE

A good practice to help bring the 2X Delegation Rule together is to create a map of the activities needed in your business, separated by the general hourly rate.

Create a full list of the $10, $50, $100, and $1,000+ per-hour tasks for your particular business.

Here's a chart that lists out some examples of how you could spend your time.

$10 Per Hour	$50 Per Hour	$100 Per Hour	$1,000+ Per Hour
Posting On Social Media	Writing Blog Post Or Email	Leading Day-To-Day Meetings	Creating An Irresistible Offer
Fixing Website	Project Management	Working With Clients	Executing Big Marketing Initiative
Basic Research	Creating Marketing Funnels	Creating Content Strategy	Problem Solving Key Issue w/ Dept. Manager
Running Errands	Car Maintenance, House Handywork	Giving Team Feedback	Creating A System For Client Success

It's easy to get busy on $10- or $50-per-hour tasks. This is often where you're comfortable.

Your brain gets a dopamine hit for checking the easy items off.

So physically, you get a reward for doing lots of small stuff—and the easier, the better. This is how so many get trapped being *busy* without being very effective!

But it's time for the next level, so you have to resist the urge and beat your lizard brain. You have to level up the tasks that you work on, spending the majority of your time on the higher-impact activities.

What are those top 20 percent tasks for you? What are the most critical things that you should focus more on—to help you not only drive growth, but to get you free and set up your business for ongoing success?

This is important to write out and make it tangible for your business. As I've mentioned, the first step to change anything is awareness, so writing it down will help make it easier to notice when you're working on the wrong tasks. You can use the table in your *Vacation Test Toolkit* (2X.co/tools) and fill in the tasks you can think of for each level for your business.

Next, with this awareness, let's now start to get you free.

> "Deciding what <u>not</u> to do is as important as deciding what to do. It's true that you can't do everything, but you can do anything."
> — **STEVE JOBS**

If you have to work weekends, odds are one or a combination of these things are apparent:

1. Your business is broke and not working—requiring a fundamental shift
2. You're addicted to your business—which is extremely common
3. You're working on way too many things—many of which you shouldn't be

After working with so many successful business owners across the globe, I can tell you that at least one of these is likely true—especially the last one.

We're helping break the addiction by separating you from the business, but to have you feel good about that, and ready to take more time off, we have to free up capacity and *SIMPLIFY* your time.

You are wearing too many hats, doing way too much. And many of the tasks and responsibilities you have are not that impactful or shouldn't be done by you.

It's not your fault that it got to this point. After all, when you started your business, you had to learn to do it all.

But, as I started my other book, *From 6 To 7 Figures*:

What got you *HERE* – to the level of success you're at... Won't get you *THERE* – to where you want to go.

You have to shift.

Specifically, you have to shift how you spend your time.

There are a few things you should completely be in charge of as CEO (and it's less than you think). Everything else you can offload.

Here's a chart that helps illustrate this:

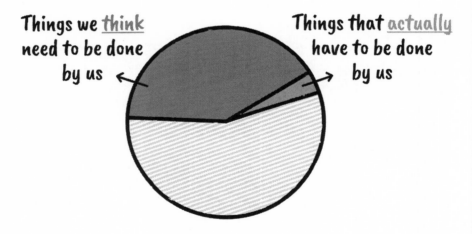

Things we think need to be done by us

Things that actually have to be done by us

The CEO's role is to oversee and drive the direction of the company, not to do all of the things yourself. Sure, you have to get your hands dirty sometimes (especially as you validate and get your operations built). But every day, you have the opportunity to decide what you work on—and what you *don't* work on.

The fact is, the vast majority of small business owners are working their butts off... but on the *wrong* things.

You've likely heard of the Pareto Principle, which states that 80 percent of our results come from 20 percent of our inputs or efforts. Well, if that's true, which it is, then that means the opposite is also true. We call this the Inverse 80/20 Rule.

That means that 80 percent of our time, energy, effort and resources only lead to 20 percent of our results.

Put another way, 80% of what we're spending our time and energy on is essentially a waste of time!

That is a wild concept to comprehend.

THE PARETO PRINCIPLE

20%
OF YOUR EFFORT

80%
OF YOUR RESULTS

80%
OF YOUR EFFORT

20%
OF YOUR RESULTS

So before we talk about growth strategies or doing more of anything, we need to talk about doing less. Way less.

We have to cut. We have to simplify. We have to trim the waste and stop working on the wrong things (the lower-impact activities that are taking the majority of your time).

To help, let's start with a simple process I do every single month to help free up 10–20 hours (or more) per week in a hurry. We call it the **XDS**™ **System**.

Here's how to do it:

STEP 1: LIST ALL OF THE TASKS

Think of the past few weeks, and list out *all* of the tasks you spent your time and energy on. Detail everything you can think of, as the more specific you can be here, the easier it'll be to actually offload. For instance, don't write something general like 'social media.' Instead, be more granular: 'creating Instagram videos' and 'engaging in business Facebook groups for half an hour.'

Even if something has taken a total of 20 minutes combined in the last *month*, include it.

Seriously, take some time and do this. Block off at least 20 minutes to write down every task you can think of, small or big. You can see an example in your *Vacation Test Toolkit* that will help. You'll start to see that it's pretty eye-opening how many things are pulling for your attention.

STEP 2: ADD THE TIME ESTIMATE

Now put the estimated average time per week that you spend on each task.

Specific Task	Time (Hrs/Wk)
New Client Welcome Calls	5.0
Creating Instagram/FB Written Content	2.0
Creating Instagram/FB Videos	1.0
Managing Payroll	1.0
Creating Strategic Partnerships	4.5

The total combined hours should be roughly how many hours you work during a typical week.

STEP 3: IDENTIFY EACH TASK TIER

Then you need to categorize each task into tiers based on level of importance. Here are the four tiers with example tasks for each:

Tier 1: **Admin** - Email inbox, social media posting, simple tech, customer service, setting up blog posts (essentially anything you can offload to an admin-level position)

Tier 2: **Technician** - Doing 'the work' of your business, such as low-level project management, client delivery, editing and optimizing web pages, basic content creation, prospecting

Tier 3: **Manager** - Team management, employee optimization, running meetings, legal, creating systems

Tier 4: **Executive** - Strategy, leading big marketing initiatives, hiring key roles, building partnerships, creating key assets (high-impact "on" the business level activities)

Don't overthink it as you go through each task. Just fill in your best guess for which tier fits for each task, as this lays the groundwork for what's to come.

STEP 4: EVALUATE YOUR ENERGY

It's not just about time management. It's also about energy management, as we want to get you in the role that you thrive in!

Evaluate how you feel about each task. *Does it give you energy? Does it stress you out and take your energy?*

Go through each line item and put:

- An up arrow (↑) next to tasks that *give* you energy
- A down arrow (↓) next to tasks that *take* your energy
- Or a dash (–) for tasks that are neutral

For me, I love creating pillar content assets such as this book. That gets me excited and gives me energy (↑). I would like to do more of that.

But doing tech tasks and fixing landing pages? Not so much. That drains me (↓).

Go through and review each item.

And now the fun part…

STEP 5: FIRE YOURSELF!

Now it's time to get you free with XDS™, by cutting (X), delegating (D), and systemizing (S) all of the tasks that you don't want to or shouldn't be in charge of. With this simple method, you'll get a lot off your plate.

The best and fastest way to free up time is not through automation or delegation. It's to cut things out.

If something isn't really worth it or essential, then stop doing it!

Simplifying is one of your key jobs as CEO, so identify what isn't essential that you can cut out or push off to a later date.

Consider these important questions:

- What is on this list can you stop doing immediately?
- **What is just not *essential* to helping you achieve your goals?**
- What things, if you cut them, would *not* make that big of a difference to your business and growth (besides freeing up time and energy to focus on higher-impact and better activities)?

For items that fit any of those criteria, mark an "X" beside them and then cross out that entire row. Those are the items we're going to cut out.

I get it, it's scary to cut things out. But every single time we've done this process with clients, we see a lot of things that are not essential or super impactful. We often find 20–40 percent of their tasks can be completely cut out altogether. That means we immediately free up 20–40 percent more capacity instantly. That's a huge breath of fresh air.

Try to do the same. Or at a minimum, find 10 percent of your time that should be cut.

D - Delegate

Next, excluding all of the X'ed items, add a "D" for which items to delegate. These will include all tasks that:

- You *shouldn't* be doing (like admin and technician tasks)
- You don't *enjoy* doing (that take your energy)
- Someone else can do better than you

Whether you have a person to delegate to already, or you eventually need to hire someone, that's OK. At least put a "D" next to those items that you plan to delegate.

That will take care of a good portion of your list, as a *lot* of things you're doing can be done by someone else, especially when you give them the proper support.

S - Systemize

Now, go through the items that aren't X'ed off and put an "S" beside the ones you need to create or improve a system for.

(Note: Some of the items you're going to delegate will need a system before you can hand them off, so you'll have some items with a D and S at the same time. This won't always be the case, but often you will want to create a system before delegating so that you set them up for success. More on this soon.)

What is left—the items that don't have X, D, or S beside them—are yours to own and keep moving forward. These items should either be:

a) High-value growth-oriented CEO activities
b) Tasks you love doing and want to keep

Everything else, you should offload asap—hopefully quickly freeing up 10–20 hours (or more) per week!

We often have clients freeing up much more than that by working through this process truthfully.

One of our clients, Joe, realized that 96 percent of his tasks could be—and *should* be—offloaded. Nearly everything! He went on to have a record-setting year and much better balance with a newborn child at home after going through this process. And we've had countless others do the same.

Again, most things do not need to be done by us. It's a mindset switch to let go and empower others. Your team wants more responsibility. They want to take on more and grow. You just have to let them. I'll guide you throughout this book on being confident to do so, but this XDS process is a great place to start.

Once you have this settled, there's a final step: go through every item that isn't cut and put a name next to who is in charge of each particular task. If you have this person on your team already, put their name. If it's yours to keep, put your name. And if you don't yet have someone on your team that would be good to own this, write "need to hire" next to it.

Here's an example of how your entire sheet will look:

Specific Task	Time (Hrs/Wk)	Tier	Energy	XDS	New Owner
New Client Welcome Calls	5.0	2-Technician ▾	Neutral ▾	S+D ▾	Brittany
Creating Instagram/FB Written Content	2.0	2-Technician ▾	Neutral ▾	D ▾	Need To Hire
Creating Instagram/FB Videos	1.0	2-Technician ▾	Neutral ▾	— ▾	Keep (Steve)
Managing Payroll	1.0	1-Admin ▾	↓ Takes My Energy ▾	S+D ▾	Aaron
Creating Strategic Partnerships	4.5	4-Exec ▾	↑ Gives Me Energy ▾	--- ▾	Keep (Steve)

After you complete this process, it's time to review and take a good hard look in the mirror.

Where has your time been going? How does that compare to where your time *should* be going? Can you see how you're working on too many things, pulled in too many directions, and not working on the right things?

You can see how many tasks you're doing, the value of those tasks, and the levels of work. And it'll help clarify why your business is where it's at!

SHIFT YOUR TIME!

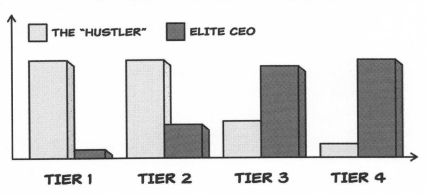

Having all of your tasks mapped out this way can be a true eye-opener and, most importantly, help you shift your actions.

Remember: what got you *here* won't get you *there*.

This simple process will help you take more control and uplevel your time in a hurry.

And continue to come back to this in the future, as your time is constantly shifting. I have done this process every month for years now, and will continue to do so. You can always find more tasks to offload.

Block off 30 minutes to work through this right away. You can download the template in your *Vacation Test Toolkit* (2x.co/tools) to help make it easy.

Once you have an inventory of your tasks, it's time to prioritize and remove these from your plate one by one. Here's a general order to help:

1. **Cut:** Start with the items to cut (X). Stop those right away to free up capacity.

2. **Quick Wins:** Then look for any quick wins that you can offload immediately. Usually there are a couple things that are fast and easy to do or delegate that will help your time. Even if it's an easy task such as posting on social media or sending out email newsletters, offload the easy stuff. That will save so much in the decisions you need to make. Do those quick and easy items next.

3. **Admin:** Then, get free from the admin stuff (Tier 1). You should be doing as few admin activities as possible. You should start to create a disdain for any admin activities. Just think of the amount of money you're "losing" versus your hourly rate by holding on to them and offload as much as you can here.

4. **Energy Drainers**: Then delegate and systemize the things you hate most that zap your energy (↓). This will help you free up so much energy to do what matters most and live your life.

This will give you a great starting spot to reduce the overwhelm and start to get back in control of your time. Then, complete everything else that you plan to offload. Finally, reevaluate your time in the same exact way again in a month. You'll see a lot of improvement, but you'll still find new ways to simplify and free up time, every time. I have for years!

Take action here and your life won't ever be the same.

TACTICAL TIP: THE *WEEKLY* WRAP-UP ROUTINE

> "If you don't disconnect from work, you'll never be able to connect with anything else."
> — **ARIANNA HUFFINGTON**

Just like you need a bookend to end your workday and transition into your evening, it's a great, simple practice to bookend your week in the same exact way.

End your day Friday by reflecting on the week. What worked well? What didn't? What shifts do you need to make? And what is your high-level plan for the next week?

By taking even 10 minutes to stop and reflect, you:

1. Learn and get better—improving each week and anchoring in the top lessons and reflections.

2. Get more clear on your time—where you shouldn't have been spending your time, what you can do better, what you can offload.

3. You set your next week up for more success by having an initial plan that is a starting spot to optimize so you can start the week fast and focused.

4. And you can more clearly shut off, knowing that you're clear on things and more "complete" to be able to step away.

Use the Wrap-Up Routine as a similar guide, and it'll be a great way to then move into your weekends being relaxing and focused.

Your friends and family will wonder what happened to you! So try it out, and take that weekend 100 percent off.

You work hard, so enjoy it.

MILESTONE #2: BIG IDEAS

➲ Productivity isn't about you getting more things done. It's about having more overall output. It's about leverage and working smarter. It's about thinking how you as a company can produce more—not *you* being more efficient or handling more tasks.

➲ Productivity plummets past a certain point. Working long hours reduces your focus, energy, morale, decision-making ability, and more. Working intentionally and strategically trumps working long hours every week.

➲ Not all time is created equal. In fact, it's wildly disproportionate. Understand the value of the tasks that you work on, cut the lower end, and maximize the high-impact tasks.

- Learn the value of your time by dividing your target annual earnings by the estimated total hours you'll work for the year. That is your hourly rate. Every task you work on that is below that rate, you are essentially paying money to work on that.

- The 2X Delegation Rule: you should delegate anything and everything that is less than half of your hourly rate.

- We think a lot of things need to be done by us as CEO. But in fact, there's only a handful of things that are really our role. The rest can (and likely should) be offloaded.

- The Pareto Principle is real. It states that 80 percent of our results come from 20 percent of our inputs or efforts. This also then means that the Inverse 80/20 Rule is real. This means that 80% of what we're spending our time and energy on is essentially a waste of time! So if we can cut those things out, and focus more on the High-Impact 20%, then we can increase our output while working less!

- What's better than delegation is to cut things out that are not essential or impactful. This is hard to do, but one of your top jobs as CEO is to constantly be simplifying. This sets you and your entire team up for more success.

- XDS is a game-changing yet simple review of your time. It helps you identify tasks to cut, delegate, and systemize to help you quickly free up 10-20 (or more) hours per week.

- Just like you have a bookend to your day, do the same for your week. Stop and reflect, learn and get better, look ahead, and plan the next week so that you can clearly move into the weekend with peace of mind. Plus, this also helps you start the next week fast, refreshed and focused.

DONE BY 10:30AM

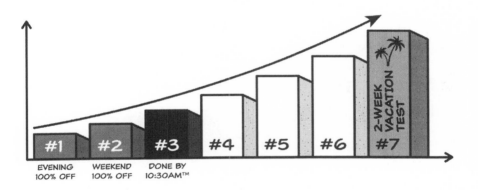

#1	#2	#3	#4	#5	#6	#7
EVENING 100% OFF	WEEKEND 100% OFF	DONE BY 10:30AM™				2-WEEK VACATION TEST

Remember, time freedom isn't the only goal. A big part of your dream vision is to also have the growth and success you know is possible.

To get both, you need the time and focus to work on the *right* things. That's what we're going to talk about next with the third milestone.

Imagine if I gave you a few key actions and an extra 10–20 hours per week to work "on" your business…

Do you think you'd be able to take it to the next level?

Absolutely you would!

With some focused time and a few levers, you'd be able to:

1. Fix a lot of leaks in your business
2. Improve your marketing and sales, driving more revenue and profits
3. Better train and support your team
4. Get your business vacation-ready
5. And scale it to the next level

So, as we get your business thriving and ready for two or more weeks off, we need to create that time. And don't worry: we *can*.

Time is the constraint you need to solve for—because with the proper time, you can achieve anything.

That's what this chapter is all about: getting you focused on the right things, working "on" the business more and more so that you can get your business thriving—with or without you.

But here's the problem.

Most entrepreneurs:

- Have way too many moving pieces
- Are pulled in 100 different directions

- Have most things still too reliant on them
- Don't have much of any structure, and as a result, there is constant reactivity
- Don't get much deep work done

And you end your days working hard, exhausted and overwhelmed—but aren't really sure what you worked on.

Is this how your day often looks—spread in 100 different directions?

No wonder it's hard to take time off or achieve the business success you know is possible!

This is what keeps you on the hamster wheel, and it's unfortunately the case for the majority of six- and seven-figure entrepreneurs we encounter. I've been there many times myself.

Then, I learned there is a better, simpler way. And the third crucial milestone on your path to freedom is to take back control of your time and work "on" the business. Because the thing is…

It's not a time problem. It's a focus and attention problem.

First, you identified the addiction to your business and started to separate yourself. Then, you realized that you're working on way too many things—most of which you shouldn't be—so you cut down on many of these low-impact tasks.

Now, you need to get focused on the *right* things: the high-impact, long-term, success-bringing activities.

The minimum to start with is 10+ hours per week working "on" the business.

This will get your business intentionally progressing forward every single week.

One of the hardest things in small businesses is to stop the chaos and get true deep, focused, productive work done.

That's what this next milestone is all about. It's the first of several simple structures I'll share with you to get you clear and focused. We call it Done By 10:30AM™.

This is one of the greatest productivity hacks for entrepreneurs out there, and will help make your ability to focus your new superpower. To get where you want to go while working *less*, it has to be!

The goal is that your day goes from being spread in countless directions to being much more focused and intentional than ever. It goes from chaos to control.

Imagine how much less stressful that would be. Imagine how much more productive you'd be. Imagine where your business would be if you have this time!

Well, you do have the time. And if you do this process, you'll be building more momentum than ever. So let's dive in.

WORKING ON THE *RIGHT* ACTIVITIES

> "Efficiency is doing the thing right.
> Effectiveness is doing the right thing."
> — **PETER DRUCKER**

It can be frustrating to realize, but you are exactly where you should be in your business. You got yourself here (the good and the bad).

Put another way...

Your business today is a direct reflection of how you've spent your time in the past. And your future success is dependent on how you spend your time today.

Time isn't the issue. We all have the same time. We have the same 24 hours in a day as Elon Musk, Jeff Bezos, and Oprah Winfrey do. **It's how we spend that time that matters! That's the ultimate leading indicator of your success.**

Are you truly working on high-impact CEO activities? Or are you wearing all the hats, including doing a lot of things that you *shouldn't be doing?*

We've already discussed:

- The Pareto Principle—which states that 20 percent of our time, energy, effort, and resources leads to a massive 80 percent of our results.
- And the Inverse 80/20 Rule—which states that 80 percent of what we're spending our time/resources on leads to only 20 percent of our results.

Now, we're going to bring this concept to the next level.

To explain, we'll talk about your time in these terms. There are the *Low-Impact 80%* of tasks that drive only 20 percent of the results.

And the *High-Impact 20%* of top activities (which drive 80 percent of results).

Let's say that you fully offload the Low-Impact 80% of your time, energy, and focus, and then use some of that free time to duplicate your High-Impact 20%.

It could look like this:

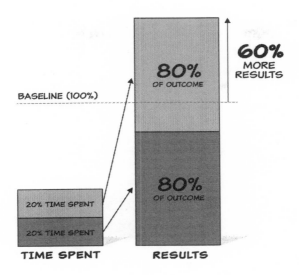

Based on this, you're working only 40 percent of the time you were working (i.e. three fewer days per week!) while producing 60 percent more—simply by focusing on the *right* things!

And let's take it one step further.

Let's say you do that again, tripling your focus on your High-Impact 20%.

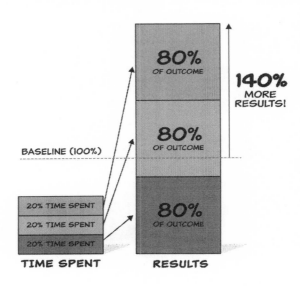

In this scenario, you're only working 60 percent as much, yet producing a staggering 140 percent more. This is getting 2.4 times the output while working two fewer days per week.

Now *that* is working smarter!

You can clearly see how productive this is. How *priceless* this is.

The goal is to fully eliminate or offload at least half of your Low-Impact 80% every six months (so 40%).

If you do this, you will continue to uplevel the value of your time exponentially—allowing you both more time freedom *and* more production.

This all begins with the full-time review and XDS™ process we discussed in the last chapter. This is essential to work through thoroughly, and it will take more than one time. Preferably, do it every month. Plus, throughout the rest of this book we'll be talking about other strategies to help free up the rest of the lower-value tasks.

But right now, I want to talk about the top High-Impact 20%. These are the needle-movers that are driving the majority of your results, growth, profits, and success.

These are often the things that:

1. Drive substantial revenue and profit

2. Help your team and operations thrive

3. Are super important but often not that urgent

4. And/or are in your zone of genius (where your unique abilities and passions intersect)

As you analyze all that you could do, what are the most valuable activities you should be in charge of and do more of?

Brainstorm a list, and use the four categories above to help guide you.

For instance, some that may be on your list could include:

- Hiring key roles
- Creating an important system
- Creating a big marketing campaign
- Delegating responsibilities (to save you time ongoing)
- Helping department managers problem-solve key issues
- Optimizing and scaling your main marketing channel
- Creating an important asset (such as this book)
- Running webinars, doing speaking or PR
- Getting partnerships and joint ventures
- Strategic planning so everyone is clear
- Improving and driving team culture
- New product development

Create a list of a handful of specific items based on your business. And keep it simple. Most of it will be related to either helping your team and operations thrive or driving growth.

The vast majority of it will not be urgent tasks. We have to reduce the reactivity and urgency, which we'll talk about more in the next chapter.

For now, get clear on your High-Impact 20%. This will lead to everything.

THE DONE BY 10:30AM™ SYSTEM

"Early morning is the best part of the day. The air is fresh, the world is quiet, and you can focus on one thing at a time."
— **ROBIN SHARMA**

To move your business forward every single day, getting closer to your huge goals and Level 10 Life, you must work "on" the business, doing focused work on your highest-impact activities.

With this, you get the important things done, make progress daily, and can drive the growth, time freedom, and success you dream of. It's simply by working on the *right* things.

And the best time to do that is in the morning before the tornado of all the moving pieces of business sucks you in.

If you win the morning, you win the day. And if you win the day, you can win the week. If you win the week, you can win the month... and quarter... and year. It all starts with the simple practice of great, productive mornings.

The best way we know to do this is with what we call our Done By 10:30AM™ system.

There are three key elements of this system:

1. Your personal morning routine
2. No reactivity…
3. And at least two hours of deep, focused work on your highest-impact priorities (High-Impact 20%)

As mentioned earlier, there are two things you can control: how you start your day and how you end your day. Oftentimes what happens in between can be a blur (at least until we improve your time and operations). But you can still start and end your day with control effectively immediately.

The goal is to work on the most important things that will move your business forward first, *before* you get into putting out fires. One of the best and easiest ways to do that is to block off *at least* two hours every morning for uninterrupted deep work on your most important activities.

Before you check your emails. Before you check in with your team. Before you check social media or anything… Do two hours of deep work.

The way I recommend this is with a productivity method called the Pomodoro technique developed by Francesco Cirillo in the late 1980s.

This is working in focused "sprints" without any distractions for a certain period of time. You pick an important task to complete, do the focused work for a set period of time, and then follow it with a short break. Then, repeat the process for another sprint.

This way, you're focused, clear, and wildly productive while also keeping your mind mentally sharp and not burning out throughout the day. Sprint, rest, repeat.

The most popular Pomodoro technique is 25-minute sprints followed by a five-minute break, but you can create the system that works best for you. I personally most enjoy 50-minute sprints followed by a 10-minute break. This allows me to get into a flow and get a ton done in an hour.

The key is to have clarity going into the focused time on exactly what you're going to work on (and complete). Then, have zero distractions during that time as you execute.

You'll exponentially grow your output if you leverage this!

You can see a video training on how this works in your *Vacation Test Toolkit* at 2X.co/tools.

For the short break after, you can walk outside, meditate, stretch, fill up your water, go to the restroom, or do other easy things to clear and refresh your mind. Don't spend it by checking the news, social media, or team communication—as these will distract you and get your mind on other things. Save the distractions for later, and use the time between sprints to recharge.

But remember: the core element is to complete two hours of deep, focused work in the morning.

If you do this...

By 10:30AM, your day should be a massive success!

And then the rest of the day is icing on the cake. No matter what distractions may come later in the day, you've achieved enough in the morning to call it a success. This way, you get multiple workdays in one. And most importantly, you progress your business forward every single day.

Again, time isn't the issue. It's focus and your attention that are the real problem. So this structure helps you get set up to win.

To achieve this, map out your own version of an ideal morning. Everyone's will be a little different, depending on if you have kids, what time you like to wake up, what your morning activities and routine include, and so on. And your "done by" time may be later than 10:30AM. Regardless, make it your own—so long as you block out time to do deep work before you get into the reactivity of the day-to-day.

Again, even two hours will set you up for massive success.

Here are a couple of different examples of what a Done By 10:30AM™ morning can look like.

Here's an example of mine:

Morning Routine, Finalize 'Big 3' Plan
50-Min Sprint: ONE Thing
50-Min Sprint #2
Check Texts & Team Messages; Plan Sprint #3
50-Min Sprint #3
Check All Messages/Email; Quick Responses
Workout, Breakfast
Re-Plan & Prioritize Day #2

10:30AM

I wake up without an alarm (typically between 5:00-6:00AM). I do a short morning routine, starting with reviewing my vision board, goals, and key principles, followed by a short meditation and stretch. Then I finalize my plan for the day (that was already drafted the day before) with my "Big 3" tasks, including my ONE Thing—the most important action I'm committed to complete for the day.

Then I set the plan for exactly what I'm going to get done in my first 50-minute focused sprint (which should be focused on the top priority ONE Thing for the day). I put my headphones on, put my phone on Do Not Disturb and in the other room, turn off any notifications, and jump into my first focused work session for the day.

Once the timer goes off, I stop what I'm working on and take a 10-minute break. I'll often walk outside, lay on the yoga mat and stretch, fill up my water, or go to the restroom. Then, I come back to my desk, get focused on what exactly I'm going to complete in that next 50-minute sprint, and get started.

After that, I'll briefly check the team communication tool to see if anything urgent is needed that day that is worthy of my third sprint. Then, I'll repeat the process with one more 50-minute sprint.

After the third sprint, I'll check all of my messages to see what to prioritize for the rest of my day. I'll respond to any quick team messages to get them actioned quickly. Then, I do a short workout, shower, change, and go into the rest of my day. And that's all well before 10:30AM!

Every time I do it, I feel like a superhero getting things done. I feel focused, productive, accomplished, and in control. And I move the business forward every single time, setting us up for more growth and success long-term. It's a good feeling to have, setting the tone for your entire day!

Since I wake up early and start right away (with no kids or other commitments), I'm usually done with this well before 10:30AM. Your routine will be different from mine, and that's okay. It will work best if you make it your own.

Here's another example to compare. This one is an example of someone who has kids to get ready for school and other responsibilities in the morning before they dive into work at 8AM.

Morning Routine & Read
60 Minutes w/ Kids/Family + Breakfast
Finalize Big 3
50-Min Sprint #1
50-Min Sprint #2
Check Messages, Prep For Huddle
Daily Huddle
Re-Plan & Prioritize Day #2

10:30AM

They read in the morning and start their day with some solo time. Then, they wake up their kids and get them ready for the day. Then, it's into finalizing their plan and doing some focused work.

This schedule is different, but includes the core elements of the Done By 10:30AM system:

- A personal morning routine
- No unnecessary reactivity or distractions

- And at least two hours of deep work on high-impact activities (High-Impact 20%) to start the day

This makes the morning a massive success!

The key to a great day, great week, great month... is to start fast.

The Done By 10:30AM™ system will help you do just that. It's one of the best productivity hacks out there (in my humble opinion). And the thing is, this isn't just for you. Have your team do it as well. The more deep work, the more productive output, the better. Everyone wins.

Now, you may not be able to do this every single day, but it's a great practice if you can make it happen. Remember the goal: at least 10 hours per week "on" the business. If you do two focused hours to start your day five days per week, that's your extra 10 hours right there. That means you will be setting each day and week up to be moving your business forward.

Ideally, do a full Done By 10:30AM at a minimum three days per week. I personally like to do four (every day besides Monday, as I have team meetings and calls Monday morning).

Think about your specific situation and map out what your ideal, highly productive morning looks like. Here's a general template to start:

Your Ideal "Done By 10:30AM" Morning

6:00 _____
6:15 _____
6:30 _____
6:45 _____
7:00 _____
7:15 _____
7:30 _____
7:45 _____
8:00 _____
8:15 _____
8:30 _____
8:45 _____
9:00 _____
9:15 _____
9:30 _____
9:45 _____
10:00 _____
10:15 _____
10:30 _____

Then, block at least two days in the next week on your calendar to start this routine. Then ramp it up to a minimum of three per week after that.

But note: As you do any of these milestones or new systems, they may not be easy or natural the first few times. There will be growing pains.

As I shared in the introduction of this chapter, one of the challenges we have is actually stopping the reactivity and busyness of business—to do deep, focused work.

During these mornings, you'll find yourself wanting to check your email, social media, and team messages. You'll find yourself looking for distractions. That's a habit.

But stay strong, and do truly deep, focused work, and trust me: your productivity will go through the roof! Plus, it's way less stressful.

Remember, here is what we're trying to create. From chaos to control. That is the shift to make.

MILESTONE #3: THE BIG IDEAS

➲ Time freedom isn't the only goal. You also want business success. To get that, you need to work on the right activities. The top leading indicator of your future success is how you spend your time.

➲ It's not a time problem. It's a focus and attention problem. So, you need to set the structures so that you can stop the distractions and make focus a superpower.

- ⮑ The minimum to start with is 10+ hours per week working "on" the business. The first step to do this is to cut as much of the Low-Impact 80% of tasks (XDS). The second step is to have the right structures to do deep work and focus on the High-Impact 20% of activities. If you do this, you can work less while having much more output.

- ⮑ The key to a great day, great week, great month… is to start fast.

- ⮑ The Done By 10:30AM System is a morning practice to do deep, focused work on your highest-impact activities before you get into the blur of the day-to-day grind. This way, you're moving your business forward every single day. The key elements of this are: your personal morning routine, no reactivity, and at least two hours of deep, focused work.

FULL "CRUSH IT" DAY

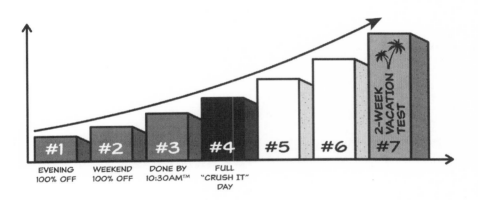

#1	#2	#3	#4	#5	#6	#7
EVENING 100% OFF	WEEKEND 100% OFF	DONE BY 10:30AM™	FULL "CRUSH IT" DAY			2-WEEK VACATION TEST

Now we're really getting warmed up! You're starting to separate yourself from your business and get in control of your time.

Now it's time to take a big leap forward.

The fourth milestone is to take one full weekday off from the day-to-day operations of your business—fully detached.

One full business day with:

- No meetings on your calendar.
- No business calls.
- No client interaction.
- No team communication.
- Nothing connected to your day-to-day operations.

It's time to temporarily separate yourself from the daily functioning of the business and see how your team does without you.

Just as importantly, it's a test to see how *you* do without your business. This is a big step.

Now, you can work on this day (on high-impact tasks)… or you can take it off. But either way, this is a test of your team driving results without you.

You pay them to do a particular job. So get out of their way and let them do that!

I know it's hard to believe, but your team doesn't need you as much as you may be thinking.

What they do need, however, is your guidance and support. They need clarity, direction, training, and feedback—and then for you to get out of their way.

So often, when we are working on things we shouldn't be working on, we're distracting our team and keeping them from their own deep work that they have to do.

With you offline, they can *actually* get some things done themselves! So this is a huge step.

Let's jump in with how to do this.

CRUSH IT DAYS

> "The best way to get good work done is to work alone."
> — **PAUL GRAHAM**

We started your deep work with a few Done By 10:30AM™ sessions. Now, let's take that one step further.

Imagine if you had one *entire day* blocked off to do undistracted deep work.

Imagine if you didn't have to constantly be looking at your calendar, thinking when your next meeting is. Imagine if you knew the entire day was free to do what you wanted, so you could get into a full flow state—where you can be fully present, focused, and immersed in an activity instead of your thoughts and actions bouncing from one thing to the next.

Imagine if your calendar looked like this for the day:

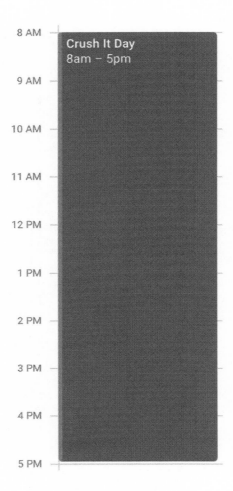

How much do you think you could get done?

How impactful would this be for your business' success? And for your state of mind?

You could do some truly deep thinking and focused work without the chaos.

Well, this isn't a fantasy. This is a key step to the path of being able to take two or more weeks off with no strings attached.

We call these a "Crush It" day—and recommend doing *at least* one day per week that is completely blocked off.

I do three Crush It days per week (as long as I'm not traveling).

I have some team calls and external meetings on Mondays and Thursdays. But Tuesdays, Wednesdays, and Fridays are typically blocked off for my deep work time.

Here's a look at my calendar next week as I'm writing this chapter:

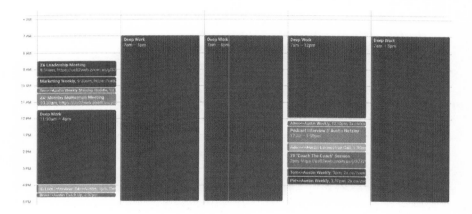

It's simple and has a massive amount of deep-work time (and freedom).

Now, I don't say this to brag. And this isn't where you start. But this can definitely be where you get to by using this book—depending on your goals and situation.

I prefer to have minimal meeting days with those times batched together as best as possible (which we'll talk about soon), and lots of deep work time to work on what matters most. But your schedule will be different. You'll have other meetings, various calls, and a different schedule, so we'll map out your own ideal schedule.

The key isn't to match my schedule, but to be in absolute control of your time and be wildly protective of it. This is crucial.

Have at least one Crush It day per week. This will lead to getting way more done in a single day than most business owners do in a week. Plus, it'll lead to a lot of positive things for your team and operations, having them be able to learn to thrive without you and start to reduce the reactivity.

And one other hidden benefit: with a clear break from the chaos of business, this day helps your energy and stamina a ton! (Especially if you're an introvert or overwhelmed.)

Imagine workdays where you're not pulled in 100 different directions. If you're in control of your time, focused, and not nearly as stressed and overwhelmed. It leads to everything you want to achieve, so let's make that a reality ASAP.

Look at your upcoming schedule, and plan this out now. Ideally, take your full first day in the next five days. Block off your calendar, move some meetings, and get your team clear that you'll be unavailable.

Now, the first time you do this, you may still check in with your team in the afternoon as you build up toward a day that is 100 percent disconnected. That's OK. But you want to build up your ability to *let go* and separate yourself. This is a new skill to learn after years of holding on to too much.

By ramping things up slowly, your confidence rises, and so does your team's. And the sooner you try these milestones, the quicker you'll spot opportunities to improve.

It'll immediately start to shift your culture to reduce reactivity and your team's reliance on you—which is a huge win-win for all.

Once you're able to take a full day separated from your team and operations, you have officially passed the fourth milestone.

Here are a couple of keys to note so you can make that happen as successfully as possible.

0% REACTIVITY

> "To respond is positive, to react is negative."
> — **ZIG ZIGLAR**

One of the main causes of self-induced stress and chaos in a business is what the majority of entrepreneurs are all too familiar with: reactivity.

When there's reactivity:

- You get frustrated
- Your team gets stressed
- Everyone gets rushed
- Bad decisions are made
- The quality drops

And nobody wins.

Reactivity can cripple a business. Unfortunately, most are running their businesses like a constant train on fire with no end in sight!

The good news is, it doesn't have to be that way. You can scale fast without the chaos. You can have things be planned ahead, calm, and focused—if you master the principle of **0% Reactivity.**

This means removing the need to react to day-to-day operations where no actions are needed that same day. This is a lofty goal to live up to, but it's more than possible.

We've implemented this into our culture, and it's been game-changing. The compound effect this makes is:

- Way less stress
- Better decision-making
- Less turnover and burnout
- Happier employees and a stronger culture
- More productivity and efficiency
- More working on the *right* activities

And here's a key point:

Taking time off becomes so much easier once you've stopped the culture of everything being urgent!

One way to think about this is what we use at 2X, which is "The 72-Hour Rule."

This rule means that if you need something from someone else, you should request it at a minimum of 72 hours ahead of time.

Nothing should ever be needed that same day, or ideally even the next day. Everything should be done, ready, and approved ahead of time, so everyone can plan their day and do as much deep, uninterrupted work as possible.

Every person on your team (not just you) has some important things to get done. If you pull them off their work to be reactive on something that "needs" to get done "today," that has a major ripple effect. Then you wonder why they aren't getting anything important done?

A culture of chaos doesn't age well in the marathon of business. You may think it helps to be busy and moving fast, but reactivity kills true productivity and output.

This is a major problem in small businesses, dramatically hurting your ability to achieve your goals.

You have to lead the way. **Whether you know it or not, you are likely the one that is leading the chaos and reactivity.** I know I have been in my company.

Reduce the constant urgency. Slow things down, plan ahead, ask for things in advance, stop distracting people, wait until meetings to ask questions, and you'll notice the culture shift instantly.

Implement some type of rule that people can't request urgent deadlines. Maybe it's 24 hours to start, but work up to 48–72 hours.

Once you slow down the chaos, then add in this next step to empower your team much more.

SOLUTIONS, NOT MONKEYS

> "The greatest leader is not necessarily the one who does the greatest things. He is the one that gets the people to do the greatest things."
> — **RONALD REAGAN**

Monkeys are problems. They're other people's challenges and the extra things you take on.

If you're anything like where I've been in the past, everyone on your team brings these monkeys to you. They constantly bring issues, questions, and needs to you.

It gets exhausting!

But it's not their fault.

> *You* are actually the one that creates the culture of everyone bringing their problems to you!

So we need to fix this. The Crush It day and the rest of these milestones will help. But to accelerate things, you have to make a few shifts.

A key thing to realize is:

You can't get to where you really want to go in business if you are the only leader.

If everyone is just doing what you tell them and totally reliant on you, then that's not a business. That's a self-employed job that is dependent on your time and talent.

If you stop, they pretty much stop. This is what most entrepreneurs unknowingly do.

They create their team (whether they realize it or not) to be followers. They unintentionally train others that they'll answer all of the questions for them! Then they're shocked when people don't magically start running and driving results *without* them—or why they can't take a true vacation!

But to get where you want to go, to create a business that drives growth, big income, lots of opportunities, and a ton of freedom, you need a team of people that can make decisions and drive results within their roles.

The good news is, you can start to train your team to be leaders starting today. This is what will bring *solutions* to the table instead of monkeys. There are four key tips to help make this happen.

#1: THE SIMPLE LEADERSHIP QUESTION

The first shift is something you should be asking your team daily. Anytime someone brings you a problem or question, simply ask them:

"What would you suggest we do?"

These six words will transform your team's *monkeys* (and your new problems) into people who start to think for themselves. They start to problem-solve, bringing solutions. And they soon realize they know more than they thought!

#2: PRESENT SOLUTIONS

Once they know that you are going to ask for their ideas, the next thing you need to do is train them that they can never present a problem without first sharing some suggested solutions.

The template is simple:

1. Here's the problem and a brief background
2. Here are some potential solutions (if necessary)
3. Here's the recommended solution and why

This way, they're bringing potential solutions so that you don't have to come up with a solution and explain it. You can simply review and approve (if you agree with their direction). This takes way less energy and time from you.

Plus, they build their problem-solving and critical-thinking skills— which grows their ability to do their job without you. When they need you less and less, they will be producing more and more.

Then let's take it one step further.

#3: TRUE UNDERSTANDING

One of the best next questions is this: *Why?*

Why do they recommend that solution? Do they know "why" you recommend a particular solution? And do they know why a particular
issue happened in the first place?

It's one thing to give a task to someone to have them execute it. It's another to have them truly *understand* that task, the reasoning behind it,
and the nuances that go into it.

But if you want them to think for themselves and know what you know
(and more), then teach them *why*. Grill them to see if they understand
a couple layers deeper than just the surface-level answer.

If they do, they'll be much more likely in the future to handle the related
issues and opportunities that come up on their own. So make the time
and teach your team. Explain things.

Help them truly grow,
not just *do*.

This is a key piece of leadership—and it will pay off many dividends as
they can handle more over time.

#4: PRETEND VACATION

The next is a simple role-play. If they're struggling for an answer and
bringing things to you without bringing real solutions, ask them:

"If I was away for two weeks and you couldn't contact me, what would you do here? How would you handle this?"

Have them start to role-play life without you. And again, you'll be blown away by what they do know and how quickly they can pick things up. They just need some confidence and a boost to be able to flex their problem-solving skills (which you've unknowingly taken from them).

Similar to Parkinson's Law, if you stop giving people an out, they'll stop using it.

It's a shift to stop training them that you'll have the answers and that they need to think for themselves. It will be a challenge for you to not just give them the direction. But you have to break that cycle.

What each of these four tips leads to is a team that doesn't need you as much, which is good news:

- For you (more freedom!)
- For them (more autonomy!)
- And for the business (more efficiency and growth!)

This is a huge win-win-win, and starts with some simple questions and shifts.

You pay your team to drive results and solutions. Now train them to do just that!

Stop babysitting them. Stop giving them all the answers. Start *leading* them.

Soon, they build the confidence to solve problems themselves. By doing so, they save you time and energy, they keep things off of your plate, and all of this adds up to exponentially more performance by all.

Remember, your team *wants* to do great. They want to perform. So give them more freedom and confidence to be able to do that. Have them think. They'll often surprise you with what they can do.

Solutions, not monkeys. It's a game-changing leadership hack.

THE 80/20 MEETINGS

> "The more you communicate, the clearer you will be, the less you will need to communicate."
> — **STEPHEN COVEY**

Speaking of leadership and getting the most out of your team, there is one crucial skill that most small businesses struggle with:

Communication.

This is one of the top causes of issues—it has a ripple effect across so much.

But if you can communicate well, you can set your team up to be clear and supported... reduce reactivity and stress... and exponentially increase your team's output.

We can make that happen with the right meeting structure and cadence.

Done right, your company will be pulsing and moving with an energy and momentum that you maybe haven't seen before.

Most small businesses have some meetings, but they're often inconsistent and a waste of everyone's time (and your hard-earned money!).

We have to change that.

A good meeting rhythm and structure limits reactivity, improves communication, gets everyone aligned, improves the culture, reduces reliance on you, and helps everyone execute more effectively.

Now, every business will be a bit different with the ideal meetings to have. You'll want to keep them to a minimum while still making sure everyone is clear and accountable.

So consider, for your company and departments, what is the ideal meeting cadence to get everyone clear and aligned, minimize reactivity, and maximize productivity?

Here are three of the best meetings that can help your team to get clear and in flow—which will make it easier to take time off.

1: WEEKLY DEPARTMENT MEETING

In this meeting, you're reviewing the key numbers, last week's key actions and commitments (including accountability), and then getting everyone clear and aligned for the week ahead.

A great week starts with a great plan. This meeting helps make that happen so that everyone can execute most effectively and be working on the *right* things.

For a small business, these are best split up to have a separate meeting for each core department. But if you have fewer than eight people on your team, then this can be just one meeting.

2: DAILY HUDDLE

For certain departments, it often makes sense to do a short meeting every workday (except for Mondays when you have the department weekly meeting) to quickly review what's going on and what people need.

This meeting is fast and focused, less than 15 minutes long. This helps get everyone super clear and aligned, pulsing every day, while helping reduce reactivity outside of the meeting.

So instead of everyone asking you about things left and right throughout the day, if it isn't absolutely urgent, they should hold that question and bring it to the next meeting. That way there's minimal reactivity, so everyone can do their deep work.

And this also goes for you! Stop distracting everyone, and bring the updates and quick questions to the huddle.

The agenda for this meeting is simple:

1. **Numbers:** Start with a quick review of the key metrics to keep everyone focused on the results you're trying to drive and help with accountability.
2. **Individual Shares:** Each individual then shares a brief update on three things:
    a. **Noteworthy Yesterday:** What happened yesterday that is noteworthy?

b. **Noteworthy Today:** What is your top focus for today? Any key things to mention?

c. **Needs:** Where are you stuck? What do you need help on? Each individual's update should only take one minute. For anything that needs follow-up, you can then plan a next step and take it offline—but don't make this a long meeting or waste other's time by solving every problem that comes up.

3. **Wrap Up:** End with momentum. Remind everyone of the key focus and principles, sending them off with clarity and momentum.

This is a fast, efficient meeting that helps team communication dramatically. Plus, it keeps you clear without having to micromanage every hour.

Now, there are a few things to NOT do on this huddle:

- Don't go off on a bunch of tangents; keep it fast and focused
- Don't do deep-dive problem-solving; create a follow-up meeting if needed to do that
- Don't do all of the talking; this is a team update
- Don't have people there that don't need to be

The daily huddle is valuable to do for many departments. For instance, your sales team can meet daily to review your leads pipeline, any actions and needs for the day. Plus it helps hold everyone accountable and moving forward.

These are especially important to keep the communication high while you're on vacation to help make sure balls don't get dropped. So, start building this into your team cadence now. That way, when you step away, they are already in flow, communicating well and covering issues without you. The dream!

If you have a Crush It day, you will not attend this huddle or any other meeting—but the rest of the team can meet.

An ideal time to do the huddle can be to end your Done By 10:30AM morning session. This way, you get your deep work in and have a productive morning, and then you can get clear with the team and start your "second" day.

No matter what time it's at, figure out the best cadence for you and your team and make it a habit. The key things are consistency, having high-value meetings, and reducing the reactivity outside of those meetings.

If you have less than eight people on your team, you could do this all together at once. If you have more than that, you may split it up by department.

3: 1-1 LEADERSHIP SYNC

One of my favorite meetings of all is my weekly one-on-one 30-minute meetings with my department managers. During these, I'm going through the top department numbers, key actions, issues, and opportunities on a weekly basis. This keeps my finger on the pulse of what's going on in each department without having to be in the day-to-day operations.

This is a great meeting to start now, as it'll help you be fully aware of each department while giving you more comfort to step out of the day-to-day and let the manager drive that department. This will make stepping away for longer periods much easier on both of you!

In addition to these three core meetings, you'll have other meetings, such as monthly and quarterly strategic planning sessions and more. But these meetings will have you on them.

So start with the basics. Get your team clearer and pulsing. These three meetings will help make sure that each department and individual have clear direction, each week and day.

Done right, your team is humming, everyone is clear, and your operations are in flow—and now you're one giant leap closer to being able to step away. The right communication structure is key to making that happen!

MAPPING THE PERFECT WEEK

> "For the first 25 years of my life, I wanted freedom. For the next 25 years, I wanted order. For the next 25 years, I realized that order is freedom."
> — **WINSTON CHURCHILL**

We're going to help you schedule a perfect week, but before we dive into this system, let's talk about structure itself.

Many of the tips in this book are related to having the systems and structures in place to make your life easier and more successful. And the surprising thing about structure is that it *gives* you control and freedom. It doesn't limit them!

Structure sets you up to win and will forever change your life and business if you use even a fraction of what I've shared so far, including:

- Stopping work at a certain time and taking back your evenings
- Taking committed weekend time to recharge and be with family/friends
- Having wildly productive, focused mornings (with deep work time)
- And full Crush It days away from the day-to-day

We have one more concept that is worth talking about before diving into your full-week map: batching.

BATCHING

Batching, which is combining certain tasks to do all at once instead of splitting them up over time, is incredibly useful to get you into that highly productive flow state.

You may *think* that juggling a lot of tasks is the most productive strategy, but in fact, it's far from it. You lose an incredible amount of time and energy by switching tasks, so batching helps to squash this.

Here's an example of what we *think* multitasking looks like:

WHAT WE THINK MULTITASKING LOOKS LIKE

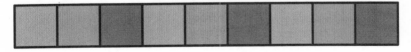

But we actually waste a lot of time and energy moving from one task to the next. According to a popular study conducted by the American Psychological Association (APA), multitasking can cause a 40 percent dip in productivity.[11]

This is because when you switch tasks or get distracted, it takes time to get back into a productive, focused mode. Here's what it actually looks like:

WHAT WE THINK MULTITASKING LOOKS LIKE

WHAT MULTITASKING ACTUALLY LOOKS LIKE

But instead of being split and jumping from one task to the next, imagine you're able to get into a focused flow on one thing.

If you batch your tasks, you can get things done in a fraction of the time—and *without* the overwhelm.

WHAT MULTITASKING ACTUALLY LOOKS LIKE

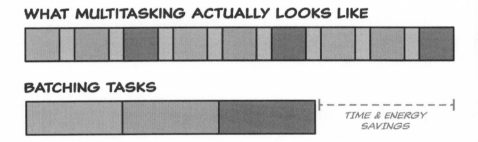

BATCHING TASKS

Another effect of this is with your calendar. So many business owners have their time and focus all over the place, and it starts with the calendar. Most have sporadic calls and meetings, which stops you from ever getting into flow on much of anything. You're constantly looking over your shoulder for your next meeting. No wonder you can't get ahead!

But you are responsible for your time. If you don't take control of it, someone else will.

So the key is to control your calendar and batch your time.

Here are a few examples:

Batch most of your meetings to all be on certain days or at certain times. I prefer Monday mornings and Thursday afternoons for my recurring meetings, but pick days/times that best suit you and get them set. We'll talk in more depth about the right meeting structure in the next chapter.

Block certain times off on your calendar (for your own tasks), and keep other times open for things to happen. For instance, maybe you keep open two four-hour windows per week that are available for meetings that come up. You also have a calendar scheduler to make it simple for people to book a time with you. That way, you know that those times will be available for what's needed, but you can get a lot of work without reactivity outside of those times. I know I'll have a few other meetings pop up (i.e. acquisition opportunities, JV partnership discussions, podcast interviews), so I keep time open on two days (Monday and Thursday afternoons) for these to happen. It's very much in my control and I still maximize my deep-work time.

Batch repeat tasks to be all at once. For instance, I planned out a bunch of videos for social media over a two-hour deep dive. Then, the following week I had a videographer record me creating those videos in less than two hours, getting 39 short videos done in that time! That is over three months of content in a total of four focused hours. Instead of thinking each day what I'm going to post, I got months done in a short amount of time that the team can then take and run with from there.

By leveraging batching and blocking off your calendar, you will gain back control of your time.

By putting this all together, you're back in the driver's seat with much less reactivity. You can decide when things go where. You minimize distractions, maximize focus, and can literally quadruple (or more) your output while reducing your stress.

This is huge—and truly sets the tone for your time freedom. So let's put it all together now to map out…

THE PERFECT WEEK

Think about your highest and best use of time. Think about your dream lifestyle. Think about being much more intentional and protective of your time, and the structures we've talked about so far…

With all that in mind, what does your ideal week look like?

Let's map this out with intention. **Let's engineer your success, starting with your calendar.** Remember…

How you spend your time today is the leading indicator of your future success.

I recommend using your calendar as the center of truth. Use it as your guide, and follow it. If you do, it'll take out a lot of the guesswork and lost energy in trying to figure out what to do next. You'll be able to get into flow. It will put you back in control of your time. It'll reduce the reactivity and distractions.

Remember, structure creates freedom.

Let's design your dream week now, so it can help you build your dream business and lifestyle.

Here's a template you can use in your *Vacation Test Toolkit* at 2X.co/tools.

The Perfect Week

TIME	MONDAY	TUESDAY	WEDNESDAY	THURSDAY	FRIDAY	SATURDAY	SUNDAY
5:00-5:30							
5:30-6:00							
6:00-6:30							
6:30-7:00							
7:00-7:30							
7:30-8:00							
8:00-8:30							
8:30-9:00							
9:00-9:30							
9:30-10:00							
10:00-10:30							
10:30-11:00							
11:00-11:30							
11:30-12:00							
12:00-12:30							
12:30-1:00							
1:00-1:30							
1:30-2:00							
2:00-2:30							
2:30-3:00							
3:00-3:30							
3:30-4:00							
4:00-4:30							
4:30-5:00							
5:00-5:30							
5:30-6:00							
6:00-6:30							
6:30-7:00							

Here's how to fill this in:

1: THE NON-NEGOTIABLES

The first things that should go on the calendar are some time for your loved ones and yourself.

These are the non-negotiable items you should put on your calendar first.

Maybe you want to stop work every day by 5PM (at the latest) to spend quality time with your kids every day. Maybe it's a weekly date night with your spouse. Maybe it's your morning routine that gets you in the right state of mind, picking your kids up from school, or a certain workout that you do a few times per week.

Add these non-negotiable items first.

2: THE BOOKENDS

When will you start and stop your day? And how can those be a success for you?

For instance, put any morning routine items like you mapped out with your Done By 10:30AM structure.

Also, have clear times and a Wrap-Up Routine of how to end your day. Get this planned, as this way you'll have a clear bookend.

Parkinson's Law states that however long you give yourself, you'll take that time. So if you don't add a bookend, your work will keep creeping over longer and longer, taking your personal time. But if you give yourself a deadline, you'll be more efficient and focused.

3: THE DEEP-WORK TIME

What times are you going to do your most important work for the week? How much time can you dedicate each week to that?

Get this mapped out now and block it off so that other things can't take its place. You then have to protect this time like gold. Your assistant and team need to know that deep work is essential and protected. This is your most important work time.

Remember the goals:

- At least three Done By 10:30AM deep-work sessions per week
- At least one Crush It Day per week

Plus, you can have other windows of time that you block off for your most important priorities for the week.

So, map out and block off some deep work time, and then do what few do: Actually do it. If you do, you'll build your dream business way faster than ever. This is key.

4: THE MEETINGS

We discussed some of the key meetings to start to integrate with your team. Add those next, as well as any others that you'll ideally have to maximize communication.

Have them at the same times each week as recurring calendars, and make them super important for your team to attend. These will keep the clarity that has a ripple effect on everything else, so get those mapped out and batched together now.

Also, note that your business and time will need to shift before it's into a perfect weekly flow. There will be a lot of things likely going on in your business that you won't necessarily plan for, especially initially, as we improve your operations, team, time, and culture. So at the beginning, you'll have less focused time than you will in a few months. Start with the basics, and then we can get more detailed over time. After a few months you can further update your perfect week, as it will change.

But it all starts with intentionality and designing your schedule now to take back control of your time. So fill that in now and get it updated on your calendar.

This is a huge step forward, setting you up for success.

MILESTONE #4: THE BIG IDEAS

- ⮑ What you'll find as you separate yourself from the day-to-day operations is, your team doesn't need you as much as you may be thinking. They need direction and support, but it helps them to get out of their way.

- ⮑ A huge inhibitor to getting into a focused flow state is when you constantly have distractions and upcoming appointments. So, the way to combat that is with a focused "Crush It" day.

- ⮑ A "Crush It" day is a full day with zero meetings, team, or client interaction so that you can get into full flow and allow your team to operate without you.

- ⮑ One of the main causes of self-induced stress and chaos in a business is reactivity. To escape the daily grind effectively, you need to limit reactivity. Taking time off and retraining your team that you aren't there to answer all questions helps to quickly limit reactivity.

- ⮑ A simple way to reduce reactivity is to have something like the 72-Hour Rule, where nothing is allowed to be required within 72 hours. Having this rule in place, you and other team members will have to further think ahead and stop having things be so reactive and urgent. Most of the time, this starts with you.

➲ You can't get to where you really want to go in business if you are the only leader.

➲ A key way to develop other leaders is to simply stop giving them solutions, and start asking them to bring you solutions. Ask them, "What would you suggest we do?" Have them present solutions, and take the time to make sure they understand *why*. If they do, they'll be much more valuable and need you less.

➲ A crucial piece of great execution without the chaos is communication. The key communication system is the right meeting rhythm. Done right, this gets your company pulsing and in flow without the reactivity.

➲ Three core meetings to have are the weekly department meeting, daily huddles, and leadership syncs. These will have you and your team clear, making it easier for you to step out of the day-to-day for vacation.

➲ Batching is a powerful process to help maximize productivity without the waste and overwhelm of jumping from one thing to the next. Do this for key tasks, meetings, and your calendar so that you can get more done with less energy. There's a hidden tax (40% per studies[11]) by switching from one task to the next.

➲ The ideal way to be intentional with your time and schedule is to map out your Perfect Week, and have it be reflected on your calendar. Set the personal time, bookends for your days, deep work times, and meetings, and you'll be set up to have more control of your time.

HALFWAY RECAP

> "Great things are not done by impulse, but by a series of small things brought together."
>
> — **VINCENT VAN GOGH**

OK, I'm throwing a lot at you, so I want to stop and recap so that you're seeing what's possible here.

What we've been breaking down so far is that the key driver to achieve everything you want in business is getting free from the day-to-day operations. By doing so, you have the time freedom, energy, focus, and ability to work "on" the business—which ultimately leads to the life and success you dream of.

The best way to make that happen is through a sequential series of steps leading to a full no-strings-attached two-plus-week vacation. What this does is help you quickly:

1. Break the *mental* attachment and addiction to your business…
2. And then break the *physical* attachment to your business and all of the tasks

To help make this a reality, we're working through various milestones to help accelerate this process. So far, we've covered four of the milestones.

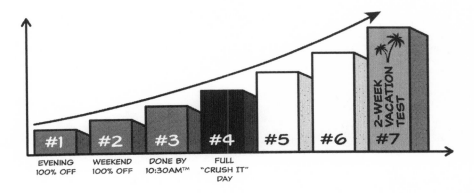

Milestone #1: It all starts by taking an evening 100 percent off, and then making this a habit. This "test" is about being able to stop work and turn it off, so that you can be present and reduce your stress. Slowly over time, we get consumed by our business—so this first step starts to shift that.

Milestone #2: Next, it's about taking the weekend fully off to disconnect, recharge, and play. To do this, we have to reduce the overwhelming number of tasks that are on your plate and realize what true productivity is.

As you've realized, the vast majority of things you're doing aren't essential, that impactful, or don't need to be done by you. So simplifying is a huge first step here!

Plus, this stage is about starting to create a lifestyle that makes you want to maximize the impact of your work time so that you work less and live more.

Milestone #3: Then, we're shifting to working strategically "on" the business and the highest-impact tasks (the High-Impact 20%). This next milestone is doing a true Done By 10:30AM™ at least three times per week.

If you win the morning, you win the day... and week. So this simple process helps you improve your business every single day, leading to more time freedom and growth.

Milestone #4: Then we expand that to a full Crush-It Day, getting more done in a day than most do in a week. This is where you really move the needle and get your team to... *gasp!*... operate *without* you. This is where things really start to get real.

And the cool thing is, **everything that we've talked about so far can happen in the first week.**

Make them happen as soon as possible because they will force you to change and help accelerate progress and fix issues.

Again, the fastest path to everything you want is through The 2-Week Vacation Test™ and this strategic ramp-up process. So take it step-by-step, and you'll see that you truly can achieve "it all" in business.

We'll bring this all together in the second half, getting you ready to thrive on that relaxing vacation in no time.

60-SECOND ASK

"As you grow older, you will discover that you have two hands—one for helping yourself, the other for helping others."
— AUDREY HEPBURN

At this point, we are only part of the way through the process of getting you free for your two-week vacation. We have a lot of time freedom and growth ahead, but first...

I have a simple request. I need your help, so want to ask if you would do me a 60-second favor?

There are countless business owners across the globe who are stuck working in their business, overwhelmed and exhausted. And this book can help show them a better, simpler way of doing things so that they take back control and live their best life.

But I need your help. My goal is to have it impact tens of thousands of entrepreneurs directly—and hundreds of thousands indirectly.

One thing that would help a ton is if you took one minute of your time to leave a quick review of this book on Amazon for me. Do you think you could do that?

If so, you could help:

- One entrepreneur avoid burnout
- One entrepreneur save their business

- One entrepreneur make more memories with their kids
- One entrepreneur improve their health and avoid a major health scare
- One entrepreneur make a huge positive impact on their community

In fact, your review will probably help *many* more than that.

So if you'd be so kind, please take 60 seconds and leave a short review. You can do so directly here:

>> **2X.co/review**

This would mean the world to me, and it could help other entrepreneurs just like you and me. So THANK YOU in advance.

Books change lives. They did mine, and I appreciate your support in helping this book do the same for others.

And with that, let's get into the next steps of building your thriving business machine with the final three (and biggest) milestones yet.

Next up: the key to unlocking everything you want to achieve in business (and where most entrepreneurs get *stuck*: hitting the ceiling!).

THE 4-DAY WEEKEND

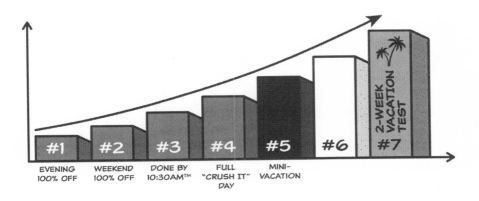

#1	#2	#3	#4	#5	#6	#7
EVENING 100% OFF	WEEKEND 100% OFF	DONE BY 10:30AM™	FULL "CRUSH IT" DAY	MINI-VACATION		2-WEEK VACATION TEST

Let's keep the momentum rolling with a huge milestone and some fun: your first mini-vacation.

For this step, you'll take a long weekend (four days total)...

And here's the kicker:

Do not take your laptop.

(You heard me right!)

Delete any work-related apps. Get your team set up to run things without you. And fully disconnect.

It's really only two business days off, but this is a big test—mostly for you and your mindset.

Can you let go? Can you trust your team? Can you relax?

If you can, it's a priceless feeling.

The four-day weekend is a common extended break you should take. We recommend doing a mini-vacation *at least* once per quarter, but ideally more.

This will keep you fresh, balanced, and always having something to look forward to. You work hard, so enjoy it!

Plus, it will further help push you to create a business that can thrive without you.

Let me explain.

A friend of mine named Dan runs a wildly successful multi-million-dollar business selling calculators. And the cool thing is, he does this while only working a few hours per week.

I love to travel, but this guy *lives* traveling. He's in some incredible exotic place 90 percent of the time. One moment, he's in Bali; the next, he's taking a van across the US.

And he's doing it all while running a crazy successful business.

So I grilled into him. What's his secret? How does he do this?

Well, no surprise that he mentioned the common things we've either already discussed or will soon discuss in this book—having great operations, creating excellent systems, delegating effectively, etc.

But the surprise was when he told me what motivated him:

> **"The real secret is to create an incredible lifestyle. The more you enjoy your life outside of business, the more you'll want to enjoy your life outside of business."**

With this perspective, he created his ideal lifestyle—and then had the clarity and motivation to push him to build his business in such a way that he could spend the majority of his time outside of work.

And that's the point of this book: To design your business with intentionality to achieve your dreams, both in and out of business.

Create a lifestyle that will inspire and push you to get free from the minutiae so you can live your best life. This mini-vacation milestone will help ignite it.

In this chapter, we'll break down a few tips to help you step away and build that dream lifestyle, including:

- The big mindset shift
- Your operational secret weapon
- How to have the priceless feeling of *peace of mind*

Done right, this will help you make that four-day break a breeze.

LET GO

> "You can't do everything. You shouldn't try to do everything. You don't have to do everything."
>
> **— JIM ROHN**

Business is an intense sport. To not only survive, but thrive, there is one crucial skill you have to master. That skill is represented by this crazy story I once read about 'smokejumpers.'

These are highly trained, elite firefighters that parachute into active wildfires to stop the spreading blaze. It's clearly one of the most dangerous jobs on the planet—these people are risking their lives in the wild to save countless others.

The story goes that 15 of these smokejumpers were deep in a spreading fire, trying to contain it when things suddenly changed. The winds shifted, and the fire started surrounding them. Being stuck in a canyon, there was only one way out…

Up the mountain.

Wearing the heavy gear and carrying tools needed to fight the fire, the smokejumpers faced the near-impossible task of escaping..

Of the fifteen, only three survived.

In the aftermath analysis of the fire, the report found there was one key difference between life and death:

- All three of the survivors *let go* of the heavy 100-plus-pound gear holding them back.
- The other 12 who tragically died didn't get rid of the weight until it was too late.

This story represents so much of what entrepreneurship is and what it takes. It's a climb up a mountain with a ton of things that can hold you back: your mindset, your beliefs, the economy, a pandemic, AI and other technology, competition chasing you, and an endless list of things to do.

In business, the ones who not only survive but thrive are the ones who *let go*.

This is not easy at first. You got to where you are by tightly holding on to the idea of driving results yourself. But I'm telling you, your business livelihood, the freedom you're after, and all the incredible success that is possible for you depend on it.

One of my clients—a man who has a $1.5 million business and a small team—felt stuck. He told me, "I know I *need* to delegate, but I'm not sure *what* to delegate."

I responded, "Everything. Let's start with that."

He looked at me like I was crazy.

I went on to explain that he shouldn't delegate *everything*—at least not right away, and definitely not all at once. But he absolutely needed a mindset switch.

He had to realize that he was in fact holding himself back from his goals and vision by *not* letting go.

And after working with so many ambitious entrepreneurs, I can guess that you're the same. I know I have been there more times than I'd like to admit!

But realize: To get where you want to go in business and life, you have to think about getting free. You have to think about leverage. You have to think and act like a CEO.

Your default answer needs to shift to NOT doing things yourself.

You have to realize that the tipping point in business happens when you get free from the weeds. And the first step to help make that happen is to shift your mindset.

As soon as anything comes up, instead of thinking, "How can I do this?" think:

- *Who else can do this?*
- *And what systems do we need in place to remove myself from the equation and set them up for success?*

This is a huge shift to help get you where you want to go. Think *"who and what systems"*—not *"how"* to do something yourself.

There are a handful of high-impact responsibilities for you to own and keep, but the rest can and should be offloaded.

The hardest part is with the mindset. You have to let go. You have to transform. You have to retrain yourself. And this book will challenge you to do just that, one baby step and milestone at a time.

So my challenge to you is:

Once and for all, let go. Shift your mindset. Cut the weight holding you back. And step into that next-level version of you.

As soon as you do, **you'll officially be on the fast track to growth and freedom.** This fifth milestone will help you start to do that more than ever. Once you do, you won't look back.

DELEGATE EVERYTHING

> "If you want to do a few small things right, do them yourself. If you want to do great things and make a big impact, learn to delegate."
>
> **— JOHN C. MAXWELL**

Odds are that you've tried delegating many times before. But if you're like many other business owners, this often ends up:

- Taking more time than it's worth
- Causing more frustration
- Slowing everything else down
- And wasting your hard-earned money

You think, *"I knew I should have just handled it myself."*

So from then on, you do, and you end up holding onto things you shouldn't be doing for way too long. As a result, you stay stuck on the hustle-hamster-wheel, overwhelmed and exhausted with an endless to-do list—and never ready for a true two-week vacation.

That was me for years. I thought nobody could do tasks as fast or as well as me. I felt like I'd be wasting time and money every time I tried to delegate. It never worked well, so I never wanted to try it. I held on to these things, and that led to me being burned out so bad that I had to call 911 with massive anxiety attacks. Not once, but *twice!*

And then I learned a very important lesson:

To get to a highly successful multi-million dollar machine and take that fully detached vacation, you must let go and break that cycle. You must delegate. And the key is, you have to delegate the *right* way—not how you've done it in the past. Your method of delegation, not the delegation itself, was the issue.

Here's how delegation typically happens. Tell me if this sounds familiar:

- You get overwhelmed and know you need to delegate…
- So you give it a shot, optimistic that it's going to work. You think, *"This is pretty simple. This person should be able to handle it, no problem."*
- So you delegate something to a person on your team…
- But it doesn't get done correctly or quickly enough.
- So you need to step in and fix it.
- Now you're behind—and stress kicks in…
- You are in a hurry, frustrated, and just do it yourself—reinforcing those beliefs that your team isn't good enough and that you should have just handled it.
- So you stay, year after year, too stuck "in" the weeds and on the hamster wheel.
- And the next time you get overwhelmed, you don't even try delegating since it went so poorly the last time.

Sound familiar?

Here's how it looks for most delegation:

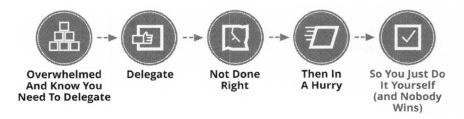

| Overwhelmed And Know You Need To Delegate | Delegate | Not Done Right | Then In A Hurry | So You Just Do It Yourself (and Nobody Wins) |

When delegation falls into this pattern, you end up worse than when you began! It took time, money, energy, and frustration—all to get the same or worse results. Not good!

But here's the thing I've learned the hard way:

> # Nearly every time that delegation fails, it's because of *you*, not your team.

To flip that around and delegate effectively, you have to follow the 2X Delegation Flow.

THE 2X DELEGATION FLOW

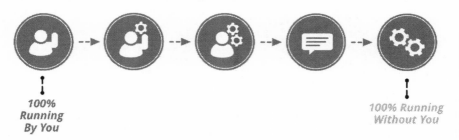

100% Running By You

100% Running Without You

With this process, you'll have much better success in delegating. It'll set your team up to do the task well, and this way, everyone wins. Here are the steps to follow:

STEP 1 - RECORD YOUR STEPS

You are already doing the task you want to offload. So, the first step is to create a simple system while you do that task.

I'll repeat: you're already doing the work!

Now just press record as you do the task, using some simple software on your computer, or jot down the exact steps you walk through, piece by piece, to create the first version of a process. This will be a blueprint others will follow to complete the task you want to offload.

Someone else can clean up the process you create and make it perfect; you just need that first iteration, so as you go through this next week start to document your steps on a few simple tasks to offload. It'll take a few extra minutes to create a lot of free brainspace over time... *and* it'll set your team up for much more clarity on what to do than just giving the task.

Most say they're too busy to create processes/systems, but if you don't do it, then you won't ever effectively delegate—and you'll stay 'too busy' forever! Spend a little extra time now or keep holding on to all of the tasks (and overwhelm). You choose.

STEP 2 - MAKE A CLEAR HAND-OFF

The second step that most never quite work through is a great hand-off. We think we communicate the task well, but in reality, not so much.

In fact, per a major study, 91 percent said a key leadership issue is not communicating well.[15]

And I know this from personal experience!

I know I spent the majority of my first few years in business trying to delegate. The problem was, I didn't give nearly enough information— or the right information at all. I wasn't clear and specific. They were supposed to know what I meant and I expected them to read my mind. Obviously, that didn't work out.

Here's what a clear hand-off includes:

Definition of Done (DOD)

What does success for this task look like? What is the end result that you're looking for?

Defining this and listing it out in detail is going to give them a clear idea of exactly what to deliver and how to complete it.

Responsibility

Make sure it's clear that it is now *their* responsibility. This may seem obvious, but oftentimes, they aren't really 100 percent sure that you delegated a new responsibility to them.

Make it super clear that this is now theirs and that you handed it off. One way to do this is to make sure all tasks you delegate are put into a project-management system with the details. Don't just mention it in a meeting and expect them to run with it from there. Follow up.

Timing

When is it due? How urgent is this, and how does it rank versus their other priorities?

We often think it's clear whether something is urgent, but trust me, unless you communicate it, most people won't know! So help them.

Share a due date and note whether it's a high-, medium-, or low-priority task. Make this clear so your employee/contractor knows when to get a task delivered.

Also, it's helpful to state how long something should take. Be conservative; if it takes you 10 minutes to do and you've been doing it for a year, tell them it should take them 20 minutes. This way, they won't be spending four hours in the wrong direction when something should take a small fraction of that.

Looking at these three elements, how well have you been doing on making a clear hand-off?

Odds are it's a low score! (See how it's often your fault, not theirs?)

Remember: Your team can't read your mind. So communicate clearly and set them up for success.

Fix this, and all of a sudden your delegation results and team performance will go through the roof, one task at a time.

STEP 3 - FEEDBACK

Now your team can take over the task—but not fully. They don't have your knowledge and experience, so they will need some feedback as they handle the nuances and different scenarios.

Set some milestones, and give them a few points of input so they fully understand the task and process. It's good to have a couple of check-ins as they get even a portion of the task/project done so that they don't go too far in the wrong direction or when they make some mistakes.

Once you delegate, be sure to follow up, give them an opportunity to ask questions, and give feedback on how they're doing. This brings it full circle and will leave you both with the confidence they can handle the task/project/system without you.

STEP 4 - FULL OWNERSHIP

Now, finally, it's time to fully release that task and let go of responsibility.

Your team is clear on what you want, they've been given feedback, they have the process down, and now it's theirs to own. Make this super clear, and update any documents as needed that show this.

Then, you can rest assured that they are exponentially more likely to succeed with the task you've delegated to them.

Here's the 2X Delegation Flow in full:

Do this and you'll be a master of delegation.

Sure, it feels like more work—and it *is* in the short term—but you'll feel the positive effects from this almost instantaneously once it's done. Try it today, and you'll see how much better your team is set up for success.

Effective delegation has a major trickle-up effect on the rest of your business, empowering and optimizing your team, freeing up your time and energy, reducing back-and-forth and reactivity, and allowing you to take things to the next level.

With this, it's important to do what we call "crawl, walk, run."

You don't expect a baby to come out of the womb and be running circles around you. Then why would you expect your employee—who doesn't have your experiences, skillset, knowledge, and intricate details of all of the pieces of the business—to do things as well as you from the start? And how do you expect them to read your mind? They can't.

So we have to have the right approach and take it one step and task at a time. Train them, teach them why, and have them learn and develop. And they'll build up over time to where they're thriving without you.

Crawl. Walk. Run.

Identify two to three tasks to offload in the next few days, and work through the process. It will take more time, but you'll see a night and day difference in your team's understanding and ability to take on the task.

To get to that no-strings-attached time off quickly, delegation has to be a major strength. Now you have the exact steps to make that happen.

GETTING IN "THE POWER POSITION"

> "Revenue is vanity, profit is sanity, but cash is king."
> **— UNKNOWN**

You now have more things off your plate, and you're ready for your mini-vacation.

To fully let go mentally and be able to relax, you need the all-important peace of mind. This is a priceless feeling and one that is hard to come by for most entrepreneurs.

And the key problem that causes that stress and lack of peace of mind is related to cash.

You can't take a two-week no-strings-attached relaxing trip if you're worried about money. So, let's fix this head-on. We do so by getting ahead financially in what we call "the power position."

What this means is simply:

1. You're clear on and understand your finances
2. You are profitable, producing positive cash flow
3. And you have a good amount of cash on hand (more than covering any upcoming expenses)

This means you're ahead financially and don't have to stress about cash in the short-term. By doing so, you can actually relax. And you can focus on what matters most, not simply trying to generate sales to hit your next payroll!

The challenge is, this is something most entrepreneurs struggle with for the majority of their career. The stats are not encouraging. Per studies:

- The number one reason why businesses fail is they run out of cash. One study showed that 82 percent of companies that fail do so due to cashflow problems.[12]
- Only 40 percent of businesses are profitable, while 30 percent are continually *losing* money![13]

Only 40 percent are profitable? That's wild, given how hard most are working.

Cash is the oxygen and life-blood of your business. It's not only what keeps the lights on, but also what can fuel your growth and freedom... let alone that lifestyle you're after, too!

To help, here are a few principles for making sure you get (and stay) ahead financially in the power position:

PROFITABILITY

Do you know your real profitability? Are you taking into account a true salary for yourself? And do you know the profitability of each of your primary offers/products?

Most do not. If that's you, well, you're not alone. But that doesn't make it acceptable!

You have to know your financial metrics in detail. Not only can this lead to more wealth, but it'll give you peace of mind, clarity, control, and more cash. These are needed to truly enjoy your time off and be able to separate more from the business.

One of our clients had a 'successful' multi-million dollar business as a well-known market leader in his niche. He was getting a bunch of PR and was viewed as a major success by those on the outside. The bad thing is, prior to 2X, he didn't know his numbers at all. He was constantly stressed about finances, so he couldn't effectively take even a day off.

When we dove in, we realized that most of his clients were not profitable. He wasn't pricing himself the right way, so a lot of his high-end projects were not only stressing him out and a ton of work, they were literally *losing* him money. This put him on this seemingly never-ending financial roller coaster. Without knowing the numbers and his finances, he was positioned to be *stuck* working and chasing money forever!

But by getting clear and fixing his profitability, it was clear what actions to take. From there, he has been profitable and growing, even during what is typically his 'dead' season!

The thing is, really understanding and optimizing your finances isn't just for those who are stressed with money. Even if you're doing well, it's an essential element to be on top of your profit and cash flow. We see a lot of opportunities to increase profitability exponentially by simply diving deep into the numbers. So spend some time here, and you'll likely see some opportunities to act on.

Plus, you can stay ahead of any shifts in your financials and constantly be ahead and in control.

RUNWAY

Are you able to focus on what matters most in business? Or are you pressed to focus on the short-term leads and sales to make sure you can pay your upcoming bills?

Most are, unfortunately, the latter. We have to get you ahead for three reasons:

- To protect yourself in case things go sideways (saving for a rainy day to protect your business and family)
- Allow you to stay focused on what matters most, not what is most urgent
- Give you peace of mind

A simple way to do this is by building up what we call your "runway." This is the amount of money you have in your business account (that's not accounted for with other expenses, such as taxes) versus your up-coming expenses. It's calculated in months.

For example, if your average business expenses are $60,000/month and you have $60,000 in the business bank account in cash, then you have one month of runway. If you have only $30,000 in cash, you have only two weeks of runway! That's a scary spot to be because it means that you *need* to generate more sales and cash in the short term to keep your expenses going!

You couldn't peacefully take a vacation if you knew you were going to run out of money soon. So this is a major piece to get well ahead on.

The absolute minimum we suggest to have is two months of runway in the bank for your business—ideally, three months or more.

This way, if no new sales come in at all, you can rest assured that you don't have to make week-to-week survival decisions and can keep focused on the *right* actions. This puts you at ease and in the *power position*.

Now, you want to be ahead for your business—and also personally. Set at least six months of personal/family expenses set aside in cash, and you'll be in a peaceful position.

FINANCIAL SYSTEMS

Systems are the secret. They are of utmost importance—especially as it relates to your cash!

You want a bookkeeper to help organize and manage your finances on a regular basis. Along with them, you'll also need a few simple financial systems to stay on top of things.

This will keep you clear and in control of your money, making sure your business is healthy enough for you to step away from.

Here are a few of the basic financial systems to have in place:

1. **Runway & Cash**: Keep at least two months of operating expenses in the bank. You can use a cash management system such as *Profit First* created by Mike Michalowicz. Whatever you use, the essentials are to be profitable and always have at least two months of runway in cash.
2. **P&L**: Get a detailed P&L (profit and loss or income statement) updated monthly that is structured to effectively review and know your financials well.

3. **Review & Plan:** Review the P&L details on a monthly cadence. Then, identify one to three actions per month to improve your financial performance.

As you get more detailed, you can have a forecast that maps out the months ahead to keep you really clear on where you're going financially. But this isn't essential to start.

Begin with the three items above, and you'll be clear and in control of your finances. This will have you sleeping like a baby, making better decisions, and getting your business vacation-ready.

Make the time, and get this all in place. This is crucial. Once you truly get in control of your finances and ahead… stay there! It's life-changing when you do. It's worth the time to make it a priority, as your future self will thank you for it.

THE EMERGENCY PROCESS

"The man who is prepared has his battle half fought."
— **MIGUEL DE CERVANTES**

By now, you're ready to take your first mini-vacation. You're ready to really start to separate yourself.

I have one last thing that will help give you some peace of mind as you do: define what qualifies as enough of an "emergency" to contact you while you're out.

This way, you can know that if something major happens while you're out, you'll be contacted. But only if it's essential.

Here's an outline for how to determine if you should be contacted. Use this with your team. (You can download the whole system to use with your team in your *Vacation Test Toolkit* at 2X.co/tools.)

The purpose of this is to use it as simple guardrails to make sure the right decisions are made, and to make it easier to know how to handle things.

It's good to introduce this to your team now so they know what to do, and so you can rest assured that you will still be contacted if something urgent comes up. Plus, it'll become much more important as you go on your longer breaks away from the business.

So, let's map this out.

First of all, let's define what an 'emergency' is: an unexpected event or situation that has a significant impact on the business's operations, finances, or reputation, and requires the owner's immediate attention.

The key elements of this are:

- **Urgency**: Does the situation require immediate action?
- **Impact**: Will the situation significantly affect the business's performance, revenue, or reputation if not addressed promptly?
- **Authority**: Can the issue be resolved by someone else within the organization, or does it require the owner's specific expertise or decision-making authority?

Some examples of true emergencies are a major security breach, substantial loss of clients, or legal issues. But again, this is pretty extreme. We have rarely heard of a true emergency requiring the owner to be contacted.

Although 99.9 percent of the time, emergencies don't happen. That's especially true if you build up to the two-plus weeks off using this process!

But if a major issue does happen, here's the process to have your team handle it.

- **Step 1**: Gather all relevant information and assess the situation based on the key factors outlined above.
- **Step 2**: Consult with relevant team members (i.e. manager or a key leader) or stakeholders to get their perspective and input.
- **Step 3**: Determine if the situation can be resolved internally, delegated to a specific team member, or postponed until the owner's return (almost every time it can!).
- **Step 4**: If the situation meets the emergency criteria, escalate the issue to the owner with a concise summary of the problem, potential consequences, proposed solutions or options, and what's needed from them at the moment.
- **Step 5**: Implement the owner's decision and follow up with them as needed, keeping them informed of any developments or progress.

Outline this for your team, and they'll be clear on what to do.

Include a preferred method of contact (i.e. text message), as well as back-up options if you're not available. All of this can be summarized in a simple two-page document. We have a template you can use in your *Vacation Test Toolkit* at 2X.co/tools.

It's also good to share a few scenarios of potential examples of what would warrant being contacted.

One thing that is good to help with this is doing some role play. Run a few scenarios of what to do when something serious (but not qualified as an "emergency") happens—such as a client requesting a refund, or a big JV opportunity that pops up.

Get your team to start thinking and acting on their own two feet. Between the key team members, they should be able to handle things. It's just better to play it safe and make sure they're prepared.

Once you have this Emergency Process outlined and communicated with your team, you'll be set for your first stress-free mini-vacation. It's a big win, so lean in and embrace it.

MILESTONE #5: THE BIG IDEAS

- ➲ A key secret to create a better operational company is to have a lifestyle out of business that you enjoy more. This will push you to take the proper actions to get free from the day-to-day operations.

- ➲ The major challenge with getting out of the daily operations is with the mindset and *letting go* of tasks. You have to transform your beliefs, which are often baked deep through experience, that things are better if you do them yourself. You have to start with your default instinct to be you *not* doing things yourself.

- ➲ With any issue or opportunity that you decide to address, don't think how you can fix it yourself. Instead, think "Who can do this?" and "What systems are needed?"

- ➲ Delegating is essential to business success. However, most fail consistently at delegation and reinforce the belief that it would be better to just do it themselves. But a key point to know is: Nearly every time that delegation fails, it's because of you, not your team. With the right delegation process, you set the other person up for success and make it a win.

➲ The 2X Delegation Flow includes you creating a simple system for someone to follow, making a clear hand-off, giving them feedback and support as they take it on, and then having them own that responsibility ongoing. This takes a little more time upfront, but saves a huge amount of time long-term, as well as decision fatigue.

➲ Your team can't read your mind. So communicate clearly and set them up for success.

➲ A key element to taking a no-strings-attached vacation is to have peace of mind. To get that, you need to be ahead financially in the "power position." This is a top stressor that keeps most business owners constantly worried and tied to their business. The Power Position means you're clear on your finances, are profitable, and have at least two months of business expenses saved up (Runway). With this, you don't have to worry about the super short-term expenses and can focus more on the *right* actions (not just survival).

➲ Another element of having peace of mind is to know that your team is clear on when and how to contact you in case of an "emergency." The vast majority of the time, this will not happen, but it's good to have an emergency process in place so that everyone is clear on what to do and when.

1 WEEK 100% OFF

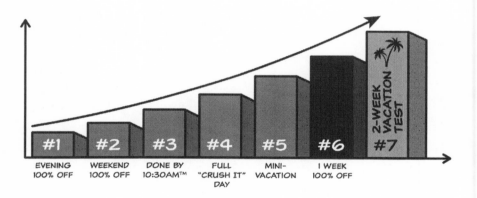

#1	#2	#3	#4	#5	#6	#7
EVENING 100% OFF	WEEKEND 100% OFF	DONE BY 10:30AM™	FULL "CRUSH IT" DAY	MINI-VACATION	1 WEEK 100% OFF	2-WEEK VACATION TEST

Imagine if you can take one full week off and have 100 percent confidence that your team and business are going to thrive.

How nice would that be?

Well, I'm here to tell you that this isn't a pipe dream. This can be your reality.

And that's the sixth and final milestone before the big test.

This is the first major test of your team and operations. If they do well here, you are set to expand that and live your dream life.

So let's take a one-week no-strings-attached break. With this, you'll spot issues, opportunities, and needs… and get things ready to truly run and thrive without you.

This chapter is all about operational excellence and building a thriving business machine that can operate for an extended period without you.

Let's make it happen!

THE KEY TO UNLOCKING EVERYTHING YOU WANT

"Operational excellence is the foundation of a great business."
— JACK WELCH

As you look over the next couple of years, what are your top business goals?

- Is it to scale big and build an empire?
- Do you want to simply make a lot more money?
- Take more time off and work less?
- Sell your business for millions of dollars?

No matter what your goal is…

Everything you want to achieve is possible on the other side of the *machine.*

What this means is that **operational excellence** is one of the essential keys to helping you achieve growth, wealth, freedom, peace of mind... and ultimately a wildly successful business that can run and thrive without you.

When we come into a business at 2X, we are first focusing on simplifying, then optimizing your strategy and model to scale... And then, we help turn your business into a *machine* with operational excellence and an elite team.

By doing so, you then have consistent, scalable, thriving operations that aren't reliant on you. That puts you in an elite position to choose your path—scaling faster, increasing profits, getting time freedom, or all of the above—and ultimately making for a wildly successful business.

Now, this talk of an operational machine may not be as *sexy* as the latest marketing hacks or showing you how to triple your leads, but trust me... It is way more powerful than almost anything else.

The thing is, most businesses struggle here.

Lack of operational excellence often becomes a business' #1 limiting factor.

Weak operations keep you stuck working "in" the business, pulled in 100 directions, reactive, and more.

But done right, this unlocks everything you want to achieve.

So, what does it mean to have operational excellence?

At 2X, we break it down into three core things: systems, numbers, and team.

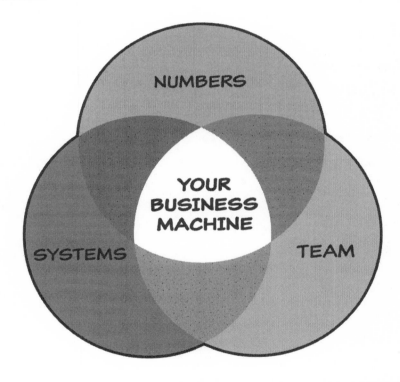

Systems are the key to consistency, repeatability, scalability, and getting free from the weeds.

The numbers are your guide. They show you the facts and are a top leadership tool.

And these two things help your team thrive… because with the clarity of the numbers and defining what success is, along with using systems to make things clearer, more consistent, and repeatable, you set your team up for success. From there, they can run the operations without you.

This sets the tone for you to take the next step and go from an operator stuck "in" the business… to elite CEO working "on" the business… to then flying "above" your business as you step away for vacation.

So let's break down each element of this, as well as how it all comes together to have a thriving business machine. But first, here's a core piece of our methodology.

THE VALUE CHAIN CUSTOMER JOURNEY

"The customer journey is the roadmap for your business."
— CHRIS ANDERSON

After graduating college with my engineering degree, I moved straight south—from the cold weather of small-town Ohio to the big, hot, and muggy city of Houston, Texas—to work for a massive oil company.

I started out as a shy, reserved, introverted engineer. On day two, the 'big boss' of our division walked up to me. He was an intimidating man, especially for a new person like me. He didn't say anything at all, just looked at me and waved his finger to follow him.

My heart stopped. I shuffled around, grabbed a notebook, and followed him into the executive boardroom. I was scared as hell as he got near the whiteboard and started talking.

"Austin, do you know why we're so successful?" he asked.

I had no clue and couldn't spit out any words, so I just shook my head.

He proceeded to map out each key step for the entire business step by step, from the crude oil process to the packaged end-product we sold to our customers.

> "We're so successful because what we do is break up every part of our business and treat each step as its own entire business. When each step is optimized, performing, and profitable, then it adds up to something pretty special."

It made sense. He was mapping out our complex business into a few simple high-level steps so that he could see the 30,000-foot view at all times.

He didn't need to be in the trenches of the day-to-day. He didn't need to know all the nuances or handle the small fires that popped up within each. He had teams for that.

His job was to see the big picture. This allowed him (and the other executives) to easily identify what's working, what's not, where to focus and what to fix. At any given time, they could see the primary bottleneck holding things back.

Plus, by treating every micro-step as its own business that could be optimized independently, it added up to a highly profitable, well-performing business *machine*!

He was simply taking the time to explain our business so that I better understand things, but little did he know the lasting impact it made.

This top-down view forever changed the way I saw business, and it's now at the center of our *2X Operating System*.

We call this framework the Value Chain.

The goal of this is to first get your business to thrive. Once that is happening, then we can get you free. Done right, things can run and thrive without you (which is the goal of this book).

> # Before you can get your business to thrive *without* you, you must first get your business to thrive *with* you.

This Value Chain process will help bring it together.

What we want to do is map out the key steps in your business, from someone not knowing you at all, all the way through being a raving fan customer.

Let's keep it really simple to start and map out your business in three simple steps. You have marketing, sales, and fulfillment.

Marketing's goal is to generate qualified leads. Sales' goal is to turn those leads into customers. And Fufillment's goal is to create raving fans, or customers for life (CFLs).

The output of this is the revenue and profits you produce. The better that you do at each stage, the more growth and cash flow you have.

With this high-level view, if you can understand what's going on for each, then you can identify exactly where the bottleneck is and focus on that. This is game-changing because...

The more clearly you understand the specific problem, the easier it is to solve that problem.

So instead of trying to fix your entire business at once, let's break it down into much smaller chunks and focus on ONE at a time.

Remember: The whole goal of what we're talking about is getting your business ready to thrive without you. To do so, we need:

1. Each department to be performing well
2. With strong operations and the right people (consistency, predictability)
3. And you removed from being required in the day-to-day operations of each department

Then, each department can run and thrive *without* you.

If you do this, you are in the top 1 percent of businesses—you are a Stage 4 business and truly ready for time off.

With this Value Chain view, we can then take this exact approach to success one step at a time.

To help, I'll refer to a simple focusing question from our Head Coach at 2X, Tom Sylvester. It states simply:

"What has to be true?"

In this case, *what has to be true to get your business ready for a two-week no-strings-attached vacation?*

Going even further into each step of your Value Chain, ask:

> *What has to be true with your marketing department to be able to run and thrive without you?*

> *What systems, numbers, and teams do you need in place to have things operating effectively without you in the day-to-day?*

Then ask the same things for your sales and fulfillment departments.

You'll need the proper strategy for each department so that things are simple, everything is clear, and everyone is focused on the right things.

Then, you'll need the right systems, numbers, and team in place so that your business is a thriving machine. Let's break this down in more detail so that you can take at least one week off ASAP.

SYSTEMS ARE THE SECRET

> "Organize around business functions, not people. Build systems within each business function. Let systems run the business and people run the systems. People come and go but the systems remain constant."
> — **MICHAEL GERBER**

Systems are your secret weapon to help you:

- Improve efficiency
- Increase profitability
- Get exponentially more output from your team
- Delegate and get free from the weeds!
- Drive consistent, predictable growth
- And get you on that dream vacation

Long story short, they're at the heart of your business machine and a secret underutilized weapon. My goal is to help you leverage them to their fullest.

Now, there are two ways to run your business: with systems or without systems.

Without systems in your business:

- Things are reliant on your hustle… and your brain (as opposed to documented step-by-step of what to do)
- There's reactivity and inconsistency
- You still have to trade time for money
- You aren't set up for if an employee leaves

- There's chaos and overwhelm because of all of the decisions that still have to be made
- Leading to unpredictable, often up-and-down, revenue

Long story short, there's no leverage, and constant work. That's a recipe for staying on the hamster-wheel of business—which is the opposite of your goal.

But with systems:

- There's consistency in delivery and execution
- You increase efficiency and have more control
- You set the team up for success and exponentially increase their output
- You can delegate more and get way more time freedom
- You can more easily optimize and improve (instead of always having to create)
- You increase scalability and profits
- And ultimately, drive more growth more consistently and easily

The choice is clear!

The thing is…

Everything you do in your business is and should be a system!

Everything.

It sounds a bit overwhelming, but it's not. **You're already doing the work!** You're already putting in more than enough hours. The only thing systems will do is lessen your personal workload.

We just need to be more strategic and intentional, turning what you already do into systems that can make things easier, faster, more repeatable—and more able to offload to someone else. This way you can get free and grow!

Even before this chapter, you knew you needed systems in your business, but *what does that even mean? And where do you start?* It's amazing how many business owners don't use systems simply because they don't know how to use them effectively or just don't know enough about them to begin with.

Just in case that hits a little close to home, let's start with the basics. We define a system as:

> **A method of solving a task in a strategic, repeatable, and efficient way.**

Now, this can come in many forms, but in essence, it's a documented way to get things done effectively. Here are the main eight types of systems:

1. Checklist
2. Template
3. Automation
4. SOP: standard operating procedure (step-by-step process)
5. Software application or tech tool
6. Video process (recording of the steps)

7. Workflow (visual representation of a process)
8. Combination of the above into one

A system can be big or small—from a simple individual process to a collection of processes and systems all together, such as a comprehensive hiring system or sales system that includes a number of elements.

Here are a few examples of different systems:

- Sales script (template)
- Handling payroll (SOP)
- Quarterly planning (combination of templates, SOP, and checklists)
- New client onboarding (automation, templates, checklist)
- Writing effective blog posts (SOP, templates, checklist)
- Setting up blog articles on your site (SOP, checklist)
- Project management system such as ClickUp, Asana, or Monday (software)
- Map of the steps of your lead-magnet funnel to align your team (workflow)
- Video recording of how to schedule social media posts (video process)
- Employee monthly performance reviews (SOP, template)

If you do anything more than once, it should be a system.

This makes it more efficient and effective, allowing you to help guide the actions people take that will lead to good results. This way you don't have to do everything yourself! And you definitely don't have to recreate the wheel each time.

Now, don't get overwhelmed here. This is where most entrepreneurs shut down as you have too many other things on your plate. But the thing is, you don't have to create hundreds of systems for your company. Your team should create most of them. And definitely not in one week.

Just like with anything, get the 80/20 right and you'll be set up to win big.

As you think about going on a two-week no-strings-attached vacation, what key systems will need to be created? **What critical day-to-day tasks are you doing that someone else will need to manage?**

To help, go back to the focusing question of "What needs to be true?" and brainstorm a list of systems you should create so that you can get free. Detail the necessary systems for marketing, sales, fulfillment, and customer management, as well as finances.

VACATION-PREP SYSTEMS NEEDED

Marketing	Sales	Fulfillment	Finance

For instance, let's take your sales department, as an example. What tasks are still reliant on you within sales? What systems can you create and train your team on so that you're officially not needed for a few weeks within sales?

Brainstorm and create those, and you'll be set to go. Plus, your team will be more set up for success. Again, it's a win-win.

You can already probably see just how critical systems are for your growth and freedom. I hope that after reading this, you never run your business without them again. They will change your life and business, if you do it right. These are one of our secret weapons at 2X with our private clients and businesses. And now it can be your secret weapon, too.

So, once you start mapping out what key systems are still needed, start creating your systems. And here's the cool thing.

You and your team are already doing the work!

You're already executing various tasks and processes. You already know how to do a ton of things. You just haven't formalized them into something that someone else can follow just yet. So we need to take things out of your head into a documented and leverageable system.

This will help you be more efficient, and also allow you to start offloading things right away. Don't wait for your vacation to do so! Let's start freeing you up immediately.

Plus, each time an issue or fire does come up (because they will happen), you will know what to do: go back to the source. Think about the issue and ask, "What system can we create here that will prevent this issue from happening again?"

Every problem is a system opportunity.

Over time, as you and your team create more systems, you'll have less and less fires. Plus, it's important to create a team culture of systems where everyone understands, creates, and uses systems. Once you do, your business will be elite in a fairly short period of time. This benefits your team, you, the prospects and customers, your bottom line, and the business as a whole.

It's a huge shift that not enough small businesses embrace. But if you're in the select few who do, you'll soon have a lot more time freedom and an elite business.

So lean in and build that business machine one key system at a time.

NUMBERS ARE THE GUIDE

"Measurement is the first step that leads to control and eventually to improvement. If you can't measure something, you can't understand it. If you can't understand it, you can't control it. If you can't control it, you can't improve it."
— **H. JAMES HARRINGTON**

Do you want to make easier, faster, better decisions?

How about getting more alignment and way more performance out of your team?

And lastly, do you want to make management and accountability much easier?

Well, here's your secret weapon.

It's something that over 95 percent of the entrepreneurs we've worked with (including countless successful seven-figure businesses) don't do well at before starting in our coaching program.

It's knowing your key numbers inside and out.

> **Numbers are the facts. They show you reality. They don't care about stories or excuses. They tell you exactly what's working, what's not, where to focus and what to fix.**

In business, *numbers rule.* They are your guide to the next level. And they help you see things from the 30,000-foot view so that you can stay working "on" or flying "above" the business—and lead from there.

When we come into a company or start working with a business, one of the first things we ask is, *what are the numbers?*

The vast majority don't know them! They think they know some of the key metrics or financials, but when we look into it, they are often significantly off. And if you don't know the numbers, you can't make objective decisions.

I can't emphasize this enough.

Without using the numbers, you are driving blind. You are guessing about where you should focus.

And you can't effectively manage or lead your team.

From my experience, if you don't have an excellent grasp on the numbers, I can tell you that you're likely:

- Missing out on a bunch of opportunities
- Making things way more difficult than they need to be
- Not focusing on the right levers
- Not getting the most out of your team
- Wasting a ton of time/money/energy
- Missing out on a lot more profits
- Making managing your team harder

And much more, simply by not knowing your key metrics.

At 2X, we track a lot of numbers to pinpoint the problems and opportunities to address. But you don't need to start there. You just need to be able to understand the key metrics so that you can drive better decisions, clarity, and accountability for each department.

This will get you managing your business from the CEO seat, getting ready for your time off.

The way to think about this is with what we call "The Island Report."

Imagine if you were stranded on an island, and you had to manage your entire business just by getting one simple one-page report of the key metrics of your business.

What would be the key metrics on this? What would you need to know?

You'd likely want some numbers related to leads, sales, clients, and of course cash.

If you have this, you'll be able to see what's going on in your business from a high level. This is what you need:

- Before you go on vacation: so that your team is clear and aligned, and that you can see how things are going, making better decisions to ensure your business is ready
- After you return: so you can see how things were going while you were out (although we recommend the full disconnect for your official two-week test, you could also get this report while on vacation as a quick update) and make the necessary decisions to drive continued growth and progress

A key way to be able to effectively see what is going on in your business and where you need to focus is with the trusty Value Chain.

The better that you do at each step, the more growth and profits you have. This is the best way to track and manage your numbers.

Now, the thing is, you don't need a ton of numbers. Simply track a handful of key metrics and review them weekly, and you're ahead of 90 percent of business owners.

Here's the process to get this set up:

Step 1: Identify the top one to three metrics for each step. For marketing, sales, and fulfillment, what are the small handful of key numbers you should be tracking that will tell you how that department is doing? Identify these first.

For instance, if you run a high-ticket coaching program, you may be tracking ad spend, cost per qualified application (from ad spend), and the total number of qualified applications. With these numbers, you have a fairly good pulse of how your marketing is trending if that's the core outcome of your marketing.

Keep it simple, and identify the top metrics for each phase.

Step 2: Learn what the actual numbers are right now. Get what the recent average has been to use as a baseline.

Step 3: Then, set conservative targets of where you should get each metric to in the short term. Now, you aren't trying to scale to the moon and grow exponentially at this point. Sure, you want to identify any easy wins and growth opportunities, but the key goal is to first get things ready to thrive without you. So be conservative to start and set some basic metrics that will show if you're doing well or not.

Step 4: Get your team clear and aligned on these numbers, so they know the most important metrics, how their work is impacting the overall results, and how they're doing. Make sure they're clear and understand the key metrics, what the strategy is, and what they own. This clarity is key so they can drive the results you're after. Plus, they know how they're being measured.

Step 5: Then, track these on a weekly basis. Ideally, you can track charts of the trends of these key metrics to make it easy to see what's going on for your team. Use the core metrics as a key central part of your meetings, and you'll have a team that is more clear, aligned, and focused on the right results.

Plus you'll have a better grasp on the business, know where to focus, and how your team is doing. This puts you one major step closer to being a true CEO and getting free from the day-to-day operations!

I know you're busy, but make the time to set this up. Once you do, you won't look back.

Systems and numbers will help you make the shift from operator to CEO. Now, there's one final piece of your business machine...

A WORLD-CLASS TEAM

"Alone we can do so little. Together we can do so much."
— HELEN KELLER

Every step of this book has been leading to this point.

The entire goal is to get your business to thrive without you. To do so, you need great operations combined with a strong team that can manage and execute things.

And the order that we've built things so far is critical. The better that you do at each step, the easier it will be for your team to thrive.

Now, let's bring it all together to do just that—so you can have your toes in the sand with complete confidence and peace of mind that your team is handling things.

Building a great team allows you to leverage the time, skill, energy, and experience of others to achieve way more.

But as you likely know, it's not that easy.

Your team can be your greatest source of leverage—or one of your biggest frustrations.

For most entrepreneurs, it's often the latter. I know it was for me.

And here's the thing:

While we are removing you from being the center of your business, you still play a critical role in your team. In fact, it all starts with you and this is the first major key to a world-class team.

You have to make the shift to take on responsibility. *You* are responsible for their success. *You* are responsible for making sure you've hired the right people. You are responsible for making sure they have the systems, training, support, feedback, and infrastructure to thrive.

The more successful they are, the more successful you and the company are. So it's your job to set them up to win!

Most entrepreneurs are so busy *doing, doing, doing* that they don't make much time for their team. But getting your team set up for success is one of the single best forms of leverage you can have—*if* you do it right.

So how do you build a great team that can run and thrive without you? Well, you need three core elements:

1. The right people in the right seat (fits your culture with skills for the role and all roles filled)…
2. Set up for success (clarity, support, and operational excellence)…
3. And executing effectively (driving results and improving over time).

Let's break each of these down now.

THE RIGHT PEOPLE IN THE RIGHT SEAT

> "A small team of A+ players can run circles around a giant team of B and C players."
> — **STEVE JOBS**

The right people on your team can change *everything* for your business.

As a result…

Building a strong team is by far one of the most important jobs you have as CEO.

This mirrors the advice in Geoff Smart and Randy Street's best-selling book, *Who*. In a survey interviewing approximately 300 top CEOs (including 20-plus billionaires) about what it takes to build a successful business, 52 percent said the single biggest factor is management talent.

Not tools. Not products. Not marketing or sales. Not even execution. It's *people*!

And the thing is, there's a massive difference between a "solid" team and an "excellent" team.

THE RIGHT PEOPLE

Recently, I hired two employees for a coaching role on our team.

One was a hard worker with an impressive resume. He came in, was hungry to learn, was a good culture fit, and did what was asked of him. But the thing is, he was a mediocre performer getting mediocre results with his clients.

That then required our head coach and me to hop in and help give him extra training. Plus, his handful of clients weren't super excited or getting great results. One of them canceled their program right away (which is rare), and another canceled a couple of weeks later. As a result, we then had to let him go and move the rest of his clients to another coach—a change that was not desirable for the clients.

So long story short, *mediocre* was incredibly costly in time, energy, money, opportunity cost, direct client impact (and raving fan status), and the rest of the team. And he was a very capable person! He just was solid at best at this job—but far from excellent.

Now, compare that to the next hire. This person was a top-tier performer. He came in and started bringing ideas of how to improve right away. He jumped into the culture and team, and was focused on going above and beyond. He got up to speed super fast, required less time from management to get ready to take on clients, and started driving results with his clients in a hurry.

Plus, he was a joy to work with for the team, was giving value in and out of his role, and really wanted to make a difference.

And the thing is: both of these employees were at the same exact compensation level! Both of them required the same amount of hiring resources.

But the end result was night-and-day. So I share this story to highlight the comparison and this important point.

The right people make all of the difference. So, the most important sales and marketing you can do is for your people.

Treat hiring candidates as your most important leads… because they are.

The right person:

- Drives more results
- Brings innovation and ideas

- Needs much less support from you
- Makes work better and easier for other employees
- Can spot (and solve) issues and opportunities before they happen
- Makes decisions and can fully own results and projects
- Helps attract other A-Players (directly and indirectly)
- Makes for happier, more successful clients
- And more

From my experience, you may have to pay an A-Player a bit more; let's say 20–40 percent more. But they're worth 4–10x as much!

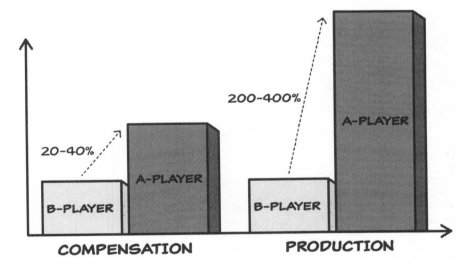

And imagine if you compound this over five, 10, 30, or more people. It becomes a night-and-day difference!

The difference between a "solid" team and an "excellent" team is exponential.

Now, not every person on your team is going to be a top-notch, world-class driver like you. And they don't have to be. But they can be excellent for their particular role!

The popular hiring book and methodology *Topgrading* defines an A-Player as: *Someone in the top 10 percent of talent available for any job, at any given salary level.*[xx]

So think about that. For a particular role and salary, evaluate if you have a team of A-Players. Are they in the top 10 percent?

The right people have the skills and abilities, and fit your culture. They are aligned with your vision and values, and are a long-term fit who is passionate about their career.

And they're...

IN THE RIGHT SEAT

I once had an employee that was outstanding at what they did. She was producing results, bringing value, fully committed, and getting great feedback.

Then, I made a major mistake. She did excellent in a coaching role (which is not easy), so I thought with her experience and initial results, surely she'll be great at another, more expanded role as our head of operations. So I moved her into a totally different department and bigger role on our leadership team. Plus, I paid her a lot, making her my highest-paid employee.

But she failed miserably. We had a few new initiatives and projects, most of which didn't turn out great, and I started to see the signs of a bad move within a couple of weeks. We tried to make it work, but ultimately both were so frustrated and stressed out from the new role that she ultimately quit within a couple of months.

In fact, this didn't just happen once. I've done this numerous times over my career, putting great people in the *wrong* roles. A few years ago I made two wrong-people moves at once, and it cost me many hundreds of thousands of dollars in bottom-line profits impact over the next 12 months (let alone halting our rapid growth and the opportunity cost of having to fix so many issues!).

Long story short:

> # You can have excellent people, but if they aren't in the right role or set up for success, then you're likely to burn through a lot of money.

And again, it comes back to you. You are responsible to get this right. (Just like I am.)

Mistakes with getting the wrong person or wrong role can be the most costly of all. It's especially tough when they're talented people, a great culture fit, or someone you build a close relationship with. But you have to review things objectively.

So evaluate your team in detail and be honest with yourself. Do you have the right people and are they in the right seat?

A key way to do this is to simply map out your ideal org chart. Start at a high level, mapping the key departments and structure. And then get more nuanced for each department detailing out the exact roles you need to be filled.

Don't just create an org chart with who you have on your team. Map it out first *without* names of all the roles you need, and connect the lines of who reports to whom in an ideal situation.

And then, after that's done and mapped out, now you can put names on it. Who owns each particular role? Some people will likely have more than one role. And some roles may need to be hired for. That's OK; list that out.

With this, it's easier to see:

- Who reports to who
- How you can *simplify*
- Who is overloaded with too many responsibilities
- Who is potentially in the wrong seat (that will need to change or get extra support)
- What roles need to be filled

So to get you free and thriving on a vacation, this needs to be set. Everyone needs to be clear, in the right seat, and set for success.

So break this down, and create an action plan for what needs to happen.

Most problems in small businesses stem from not having clarity. So this is a worthwhile process to do for you and for your team.

And it's important to note. One of the core things I want you to realize with this book is that simplicity is crucial. It's essential for your team, time, focus, and growth.

Complexity is the enemy of small businesses.

With complexity, you are overwhelmed and can't get free, and your team is overwhelmed and can't perform. Your business is held back dramatically by doing so.

So reduce the moving pieces. Cut things out, simplify, and make your business much easier to win. This is hard to do, but a necessary skill to master as CEO.

Simple scales.

SET UP TO WIN

I hate to break it to you, but hoping you can have a team of unicorns that can do everything you know how to do for a very low cost is not going to happen. But…

What you can do is hire strong people and make them *outstanding* with the right structure and support.

That's what we need to do here.

As I started the chapter, even as we remove you from being the center of your business, you play a major role on your team. You set the tone. You create the culture. And you have to shift your mentality to take responsibility and set your team up for success.

Think of McDonald's. They have the training, structure, and systems in place to make it easy for any average Joe off the street to make a Big Mac just as well as anyone else! And they can do so with speed and accuracy. McDonald's has mastered making things turnkey, and it's one of the key reasons why they're one of the top companies in the world.

Now, you don't have to be McDonald's to use this mentality and take *responsibility* for your team's success. Put the training, systems, and infrastructure in place so you can hire *good* people and **make them great!**

It is *your* responsibility to make things so clear and easy that they cannot fail!

I know what you're thinking, *"But Austin, I don't have the time to do any of those things."*

That's why the book is in this order—to show you how to simplify, get clear, and take back control of your time first so you can work "on" the business (important things such as systems, team, and growth). Because you *do,* in fact, have time! You're just not using it properly.

Imagine what it would mean for your business long-term if your team was properly trained and supported.

It's a priceless shift to make... and one that will get you vacation-ready and *keep* you free from the weeds.

And that leads us to the critical piece that helps set them up for success with one special tool.

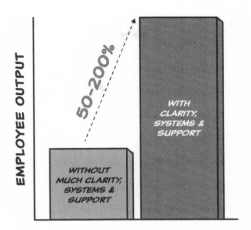

Do you ever get frustrated that your team just isn't performing? You know they can do it, and you know they *want* to succeed. But what's missing?

In nearly every small business we've worked with, we see these team issues:

- They aren't clear on exactly what is expected of them (even if it's clear to you).
- They aren't empowered and given full ownership over their work (fearing that you are going to fix it anyway).
- They're pulled in too many directions (most of which aren't their highest-impact responsibilities).
- They aren't trained or supported well enough to know what to do.
- And they aren't held accountable.

One thing that helps change all of that is a Role Scorecard. This is the centerpiece for every role, and needs to be for your team, as well.

We use it to get clear before and during the hiring process, and every month thereafter for as long as they're a part of your team. It's the roadmap for their role and helps drive clarity and better communication so that each employee can thrive.

There are four core elements of the Role Scorecard.

ROLE SCORECARD #1 - RESPONSIBILITIES

First, define the top responsibilities of the role. What tasks and duties will they lead and own?

For instance, your executive assistant might have the following top role responsibilities:

1. Communications & Calendar Management (handling various inboxes and scheduling)
2. Business Admin Support
3. Team Culture/Communication Support
4. Personal Assistant Supporting Tasks (helping outside of business tasks)

Then for each, you can include a few sub-bullets that further define the role and what's expected of them to own. This way, they have absolute clarity of what's expected of them.

Next, every role needs…

ROLE SCORECARD #2 - KEY METRICS

> # How can employees win the game if they don't know how they're being measured?

They can't and they won't.

Get clear on the top handful of metrics for their role, make sure they're aligned, and then track and review these results with them during your monthly one-on-one check-ins.

The numbers take out a lot of the emotions and have you both see the facts. This helps a ton to lead your employees fairly and hold them accountable. From here, you can see objectively how they're performing and make a game plan for how to improve.

Now, sometimes it's clear what the metrics that somebody impacts are (i.e. a sales rep having a sales closing rate). But many times it's not directly clear, such as with an executive assistant or operations role. That doesn't mean you shouldn't track the numbers!

Every role should be clear on how their work is making an impact and how their work leads to the company's overall goals and success, even if it's indirectly.

So think, what key metrics is their work contributing to? How can you quantify things so that they're super objective, and not left up for interpretation?

Tracking the metrics feels like work at the beginning, but it's game-changing and ultimately helps employees drive big results in their roles. So, define the top metrics for each role, and get them aligned on them. Then track and review these in detail, and your results will rise to the next level if you have the right people in place.

ROLE SCORECARD #3 - THE MONTHLY FOCUS ITEMS

The next piece is to have a clear monthly plan. What are the top specific projects or initiatives that they should be focusing on for the month ahead (outside of their normal day-to-day operations)? What key systems can they create or improve?

Get them clear on the top priorities, and they'll be able to be super focused throughout the month, making big tangible progress.

Be conservative with this, as they have a lot of day-to-day responsibilities already. But with a handful of focused projects, they'll be improving their department and role results in the short and long term.

ROLE SCORECARD #4 - THE MONTHLY 1-1 REVIEW

And the final piece is to bring it all together with a full-on monthly performance review. For this, you'll use the Role Scorecard as your centerpiece.

This opens the lines of communication for both sides, and gets you and your employees on the same page so you can help them optimize their performance.

The general order of the review is:

1. A self-assessment completed by the employee before the meeting on the Role Scorecard, as well as brainstorming key items for the next month's success
2. The manager's review and comments assessing the last month, and brainstorming improvements and next month's success
3. A one-on-one meeting with their manager to discuss their full Role Scorecard in detail and get them clear on the month ahead

With this structure, you clear the air, hold them accountable, get re-aligned, and help them improve—each and every month.

Imagine what's possible if they get better and better every single month with this clarity, accountability, and support. They can become unstoppable!

With Numbers, Support, Clarity, Accountability & Monthly 1-1 Feedback

Typical Employee Progression

These are some of the most valuable meetings of your entire month, so make them a habit starting right away.

This helps you, helps them, improves their role and ownership, and gets you one major step closer to having your team thrive without you in the day-to-day.

Use our Role Scorecard template as your guide because the right setup makes this so much easier. You can get access to the spreadsheet template we use in your *Vacation Test Toolkit* (2X.co/tools) and start using that now.

TACTICAL TIP: YOUR UPDATED RESPONSIBILITY LIST

At this time, you're almost set to take that first entire week off.

Before you do, to set yourself up for success, we need to make sure once more that all of your responsibilities are covered by someone.

A simple way to do this is to list out what day-to-day functions you currently own that will need to be done while you're out. And this is best to list out by department, as it'll be easier to see who to offload these to.

So, list out your current responsibilities for:

1. Marketing
2. Sales
3. Fulfillment
4. Other Operations (including finance)

What are all of the things that you do on any given week that will still need to get done while you're out?

For instance, here's an example of the list that one of our 2X clients made before he took his first full week off (to go run a half Ironman race and then do a family vacation).

Current tasks

Marketing
- Video script writing (shorts)
- Video recording (shorts)
- Partner outreach
- Partner meetings
- Webinar prep
- Webinar hosting live
- MWF Instagram stories answering

Sales
- My "hot leads" Inbox
- Reviewing sales metrics; discussing with leadership
- Occasional program sales calls

Fulfillment
- Bi-weekly group program call
- Weekly office hours Q&A call

Operations
- Payroll
- Banking
  - Paying off credit cards
- Team meeting
  - Prep
  - Host
- Monthly 1-1s w/ direct reports (4)
- My email inbox

By having this map, it was clear what final things he needed to train his team on to be able to back him up temporarily. He then felt fully prepped and confident—and didn't work once.

Then, for some of these things, he permanently offloaded upon his return. And more he will continue to offload in the coming months as his role continues to shift to bigger things and less in the day-to-day.

So fill this in now, make a game plan to back you up by training them on what they need to know, and go take that full week off.

You will be happy you did!

MILESTONE #6: THE BIG IDEAS

⮑ Operational excellence is a crucial key to achieving your business goals. Done right, this will help you have consistency, predictability, and your business to run and thrive without you. The bad news is, this is a top limiting factor in most small businesses.

⮑ Three core elements of operational excellence break down into systems, numbers, and your team. If you get each of these right, you'll be set for high-performing and profitable operations (without the chaos and your constant involvement).

⮑ As CEO, you need to see the 30,000-foot view at all times. The best way to do that is with the Value Chain, breaking your customer journey into a series of steps. With this, you can more easily address challenges and opportunities in individual chunks, making it easier to manage and guide your team.

⮑ Before you try to get your business to thrive without you, you must first get your business to thrive with you. So don't be afraid to get hands-on and get things proven and validated before systemizing and delegating to other people. Validate, get the result, and then work to systemize and scale from there.

⮑ Use the focusing question of "What has to be true?" to help you get clear on how to get your marketing, sales, fulfillment and finance departments set up to run and thrive without you.

⊃ Everything in your business is, and should be, a system. Systems will help you get more done, more efficiently and consistently, and set your team up for success as you delegate things. They are a crucial piece to master for a high-performing business—and your time freedom.

⊃ You and your team are already doing the work. You just need to document what you do and leverage systems to make that task easier, more efficient, and more effective long-term.

⊃ The numbers are the guide. They show you what's working, what's not, where to focus and what to fix. They take out the story and emotions, and show the facts of what's really going on. As a result, they're one of your best management tools as CEO. They help you make better decisions, lead your team, and hold them accountable.

⊃ Track your key metrics for each major step of your Value Chain. By seeing this, you can see the 30,000-foot view of your business, and know where to focus your efforts and energy. This also helps your team get clear and aligned, all working to improve the key metrics.

⊃ The third pillar of your business machine is a world-class team. This is a key point of leverage, but only if it's done right. To make sure you do have the right team, there are three key elements: You have the right people, in the right role, and set up for success.

⊃ The right people make all of the difference. So, the most important sales and marketing you can do is for your people. Treat hiring candidates as your most important leads… because they are.

⊃ You can have excellent people, but if they aren't in the right role or set up for success, then you're likely to burn through a lot of money. Make sure you have people in a role that they can thrive in and you take the time to support them. This will save you so much time long-term.

⊃ Simple scales. Complexity is the enemy of small businesses. Keep things as simple as possible to reduce the moving pieces. This sets everyone, and the business overall, up to win. Simplifying and cutting out the non-essential is a key part of your role as CEO. This way, you set your team up for the most success by removing the waste and overwhelm.

⊃ It is your responsibility to make things so clear and easy that your team cannot fail! With this view, you're giving them the clarity, systems, training and support so that they can thrive without you. Again, this takes more time upfront, but saves you an incredible amount of time long-term. Invest in your people and they'll return much more.

⊃ A key team system that will help you better lead each employee is the Role Scorecard. This is a tool reviewed on a monthly basis that helps open the conversation for performance, accountability, key metrics, and projects for the month. By using this, they're clear, aligned, supported, and held accountable—thus getting important things done and improving every month.

THE 2-WEEK VACATION TEST

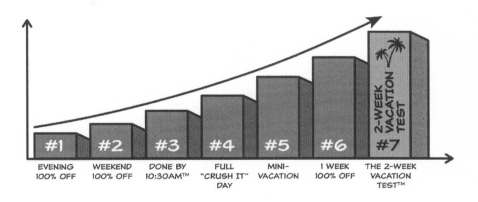

#1	#2	#3	#4	#5	#6	#7
EVENING 100% OFF	WEEKEND 100% OFF	DONE BY 10:30AM™	FULL "CRUSH IT" DAY	MINI-VACATION	1 WEEK 100% OFF	THE 2-WEEK VACATION TEST™

You made it! Now it's time for the real deal. It's time for your 2-Week Vacation Test!

This is the true test of your business—does it thrive? Or struggle?

It's time to find out. After this test, it will be clear just how strong and healthy your business is.

After taking this time off, one of four outcomes will happen:

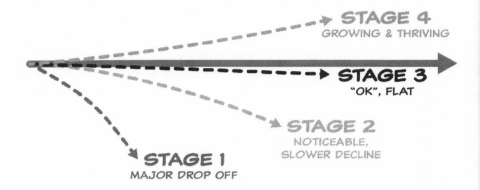

- **Stage 1**: Your business would fail pretty quickly without you. You pretty much *are* the business.
- **Stage 2**: Your business would slowly fail and start to fall apart without your direction and work. Your business is still centered around you.
- **Stage 3**: Things would be able to operate fine without you for a few weeks but not grow. Your business isn't reliant on you short term, but it's not advancing much while you're out.
- **Stage 4**: Your business would still thrive and be able to grow without you! This is where you want to be.

If you implement things step by step to this point so far, you're more clear and confident in your team… and they're set up to thrive.

Remember, you'll be taking two full weeks off from your business. The goal is to be *fully disconnected* from work.

Just like it takes some time to truly get into a deep workflow, it will take some time to truly unplug. Our minds are *going* all of the time, so it will likely take a couple of days to stop that *busyness*. But done right, this will be a beautiful time to recharge, reflect, and let your team run the show. They will learn and grow so much—as will you… you just have to stay strong.

Building up toward this with the ramp-up process will help make it a breeze. By following each milestone, you'll be chomping at the bit to go on vacation and let your team shine (instead of being afraid like you likely were at the beginning of this book!).

And this is where something special happens. Once your business can thrive at this milestone, you'll officially prove you can detach yourself from your business.

This will put you working "on" and flying "above" the business—where most of your time should be as a CEO.

Once you pass with a Stage 4 thriving business, you officially are among the elite entrepreneurs where:

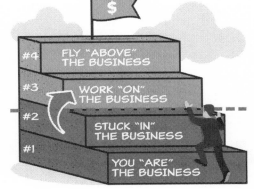

- You can work as much or little as you want (on things you enjoy)
- Your team and operations are set and thriving (without you!)
- Your team has more autonomy and ownership (leading to more satisfaction and growth)
- You are recharged and energized (and no longer burnt out and overwhelmed)

- You can see your business so much more clearly and strategically (seeing what to do to improve)
- You are exponentially more likely to scale—as your business is no longer dependent on your hours

And as a result, growth and big success become substantially easier!

So it's crucial to get here and do it right.

Let's get you set up to make that happen!

IMPLEMENTING YOUR 2-WEEK VACATION TEST

> "The more prepared you are, the luckier you will be."
> — BENJAMIN FRANKLIN

With a great sales system, there are systems for before, during, and after a sale to maximize conversions. The same is going to be true for your two-week vacation.

To have the best, most relaxing and successful time off, we need to get you and your team prepared before you go. After you do that, I'll share more about what to do while you're off... And lastly, how to handle things upon your return.

So let's break those down now.

THE PRE-VACATION PROCESS

BEFORE YOU GO: CREATING THE RULES IN ADVANCE

Here is a list of ideas and notes to help you get ready for a stress-free vacation.

1. Set some general guidelines so that your team is clear on decisions that can be made. Train them weeks in advance to think for themselves, bringing you solutions not "monkeys," and start to think more on their own.

2. Set a small budget that they don't have to run by you. For example, if they can fix an issue or need something that costs less than $100, then they don't need to ask you—just make the decision they think is best.

3. Hold off on any major business decisions or moves. Don't do any big marketing initiatives or new products or anything that could increase the chances of needing you. It should be "business as usual," operating the typical day-to-day without anything major or new happening.

4. Get your team and anyone that needs to know that you'll be out updated and prepared. This includes your full team, including contractors and agencies, but also clients/customers (if applicable).

5. What are all the ways that people communicate with you? And how can those be handled in your absence? For instance, I have my social messages and email inboxes that my assistant

handles. Those are my primary communication channels for prospects, my network, and PR opportunities—so my assistant can handle those easily. My internal team communications are on Slack, but my team knows I won't be checking those. So think of your communication. Are there any channels that are required to be checked or forwarded to someone while you're off so that no balls are dropped?

6. Set up an autoresponder to let people know that your responses will be slower or what the criteria will be for your time off.

7. Block off some time on your calendar for right *before* you leave. This will help you get caught up on the most important things, as there will be a few key things to finish before you're off. Weeks in advance, you may not know what those are just yet, so it'll be good to plan ahead and expect for you to need that deep work time on the last couple of days. This will help set your team and business up to thrive without you.

8. Also, before you leave, set meetings with your key team members on the calendar for right *after* you're back to get all caught up and review things right once you return. Have them come prepared with an update, key issues, and lessons. Get this on the calendar before you leave so that there isn't reactivity when you return and they're prepared.

9. And don't forget to train your team on the Emergency Process and what qualifies as an emergency to contact you. Remember, 99.9% of decisions can wait a few days for you to get back, but there could definitely be an urgent issue pop up. So use our guide for that.

THE 2-WEEK VACATION TEST PREP CHECKLIST

Is it still scary to think about taking a full 2+ week, no-strings-attached vacation? Don't worry. You will build confidence with each milestone. Plus, here is a checklist of what needs to happen to officially have your business vacation-ready.

Use this to not only check how you're doing now, but as a guide for what to prepare for over the coming weeks and months as you build the health of your business.

THE VACATION-PREP CHECKLIST:

1. Ahead financially in the "power position" (two-plus months of business cash saved)
2. Marketing is able to run effectively without you
3. Sales can be generated and run effectively without you
4. Fulfillment is able to run effectively without you
5. Finance/payments are able to run without you (both incoming and necessary outgoing payments, i.e. payroll)
6. All of your day-to-day tasks and responsibilities are backfilled so that no balls get dropped
7. Team is clear on who owns what with clear chain of command and decision-making hierarchy for your time out
8. Communication is all set for while you're off (team meetings and communication, inboxes and essential channels, proper people notified)
9. Tracking and reporting is set with clear visibility of key metrics and projects

10. Defined contingency plan set and clear (in case of unexpected situations, challenges, opportunities, or emergencies) so the team knows when and how to contact you

11. Team and you are prepared to track lessons, issues, and opportunities to make for most effective time off (including debriefing after return)

Get these ready and you're set for an incredible break.

There is a full printable checklist in your *Vacation Test Toolkit* at <u>2X.co/tools</u>. Print this off, and we'll use this as your guide to get ready to go.

THE DURING-VACATION PROCESS

Now it's finally time!

It's time to go. Take off.

Let go. Trust your team. They'll survive!

Sure, they'll learn. Sure, it'll be hard for you at first. Sure, there *will* without a doubt be a few fires or things not done perfectly the first time or two. But trust me—if you follow this process I've laid out for you, you'll be set up to win.

And I can tell you: the feeling of *freedom* and actually letting go is priceless. It's something that entrepreneurs can often forget what it even feels like. But this Vacation Test process brings it back.

The feeling of fully disconnecting will likely take a few days.

Our body carries so much tension and angst with the stress of a small business (and life). But once you hit the point where your mind stops going 100 miles per hour and you can fully relax and just be, then you've made it. That's freedom.

You will be less stressed, more present, and be learning a lot.

Take advantage of the time off. As with anything, being intentional leads to the most success. Identify what your top area of focus needs to be, and make it happen.

For instance, maybe a key thing for you is to catch up on high-quality family time. Focus on that and making memories.

Or maybe your focus is to fully recharge from burnout. Go all in and do that.

Or maybe it's to create, play, have fun, and feel *alive* again. Do that.

Or maybe there's some not-so-exciting things that you have been putting off (like taxes or a big house project) that are like a dark cloud over your head that you need to get done. Great, do that.

Regardless of what needs your attention, take full advantage of this time off. Be intentional, defining what a "massive success" will be for your time off. Simply answer the question:

What will be a 10 out of 10 success for this time off?

Simplify things down to the essence of what a successful break is for you. Keep it simple with a list of one to three core things. Write that down ahead of time, then go make it happen.

WHILE YOU'RE OFF

Have your team and especially your direct reports create a log of issues and opportunities that pop up while you're out.

- What issues happened?
- What questions/needs do they have for you for when you're back?
- What systems need to be created or improved?
- What are the key gaps and issues that showed up?
- What can be improved for the next 2-Week Vacation Test?
- What were the top wins during the time off?

Have them keep a log of these things individually, and ask them to send that report to you when you're back to review on your meeting with them.

You will learn a lot during this time as well. You'll learn about yourself. You'll learn about where you're addicted to your business. You'll learn about your team and how you spend your time. You'll learn about the biggest issues and gaps. You'll learn about what you really want.

It's a priceless process. So lean in and take full advantage, keeping some active notes of what comes up.

Here are a few categories for your own notes:

> **Brain-Dump Ideas:** I personally love to have my own brainstorm list of things that come to mind while I'm on vacation. You always see things with fresh eyes by being away, so it's good to have a "brain dump" journal or document to list out the ideas that spring to your rested mind.
>
> You might think of opportunities of how to simplify, what to tweak, what decisions need to be made, actions to take, growth levers to focus on, or big ideas to take your company and vision to the next level. Remember to write these down when you think of them, or you might lose them over your next oceanside margarita!
>
> **Addictions:** This is also a perfect time to spot your attachment to your business.
>
> You're likely (whether you know it or not), addicted to your business. You're addicted to the busyness. You're maybe addicted to social media, or being needed, or checking email.
>
> I know it sounds crazy, but we all are addicted to some things that we don't even realize!
>
> After taking lots of time off, I realized that I'm addicted to Slack communication with my team. I'm addicted to responding quickly.

It used to take me three to four days to slow my mind and actually stop thinking about business because I had an urge to always feel busy and productive. To always be checking things. Then, I learned how to shift it—and it especially helps by writing it down. Again, awareness is the first step.

Create a list of what urges you have and what you're addicted to. Then, plan how you can address those head-on. For instance, I now use an app to block a couple of apps that I was checking too much in the morning (like Slack) and that helped retrain me to not check it on my phone, which has been huge.

This is an eye-opening process as you step away.

Time Shifts: You now have a new appreciation for freedom and a new lens on your time. You'll see how so much of your time is being spent on things that don't work or don't matter. You'll see more clearly where you should be focusing more.

Utilize this insight while it's fresh to list any changes you might want to try making with how you structure and spend your time. Make those shifts while it's clear before you go back to "business as usual."

Lessons: Also keep a log of what you learn by taking time off. What are the key lessons? What do you learn about yourself, your team, and business success? Do a recap of your biggest insights from this, so that you anchor in those lessons to be a better, more-aware CEO in the future.

One of the many goals of this vacation test is to make your business substantially better. By reflecting properly, you'll do just that.

And a very important point is:

Never leave one vacation without scheduling the next one!

It's always good to have something that you (and your spouse/family/friends) can look forward to. You work hard for a reason, so enjoy it!

As you work the process, you'll see that it's easier—and in fact more valuable than you ever thought possible.

Yes, again, some things will fail. There will be some issues. But you'll learn and get substantially better, hopefully making every break more smooth than the last.

Plus, you'll keep yourself centered and realigned on what is most important. It's a full-on reset in so many ways, so take full advantage.

THE DURING VACATION CHECKLIST

1. Define your 10-out-of-10 success—and be intentional about achieving it
2. Have your team create a log of issues, questions, needs, and fixes

3. Use the time off to brainstorm ideas, improvements, and opportunities
4. Identify your urges and what you're addicted to, plus how you can address those
5. Detail out how your time needs to shift after taking a step back
6. Start a "Key Lessons Learned" list
7. Set your next big vacation or time off on the calendar

THE POST-VACATION PROCESS

WHEN YOU'RE BACK

I've mentioned it a few times, but I'll mention it again:

There *will* be issues. There will be fires. There will be a lot of things that didn't go perfectly as planned, or that you would have done differently. It'll be easy to spot the negatives and even consider that taking time off was a bad decision. Don't freak out. This is normal.

First off, you should expect issues, so that you're not thrown off when they do happen.

Secondly, now is a great time to identify those issues so that you can improve them while it's fresh—and with a relaxed mind, to boot. Create a list based on what you and your team all see. Look at this list as good news of clear things to make your business much healthier.

Once you have the list of issues and opportunities, it's time to go take some actions. Create and improve systems, and use this time to lean in and get further and further removed from the day-to-day.

It's a precious time to make some of these changes permanent! Do not get sucked back in the daily grind and have things be like they were. That's the worst thing you can do.

You never want to waste a good vacation.

> # By being strategic and intentional, the 2+ weeks will not only be about survival. They will instead be a fundamental up-leveling for your entire business.

This is why the 2-Week Vacation Test is one of the single best things you can do for your success (not just your freedom).

Here are a few things to consider and do upon your return:

1. Meet with each key team member to review the time off, lessons learned, fixes, and improvements.
2. Give your team more responsibility ongoing—if they showed they can do a particular thing, give it to them. Let them run with it as you do less yourself.
3. Train and teach your team—this is a golden time to help them improve, understand why things happen a particular way or how to do things, and fix issues head-on.
4. Quick wins and clean up—there will definitely be some simple, quick fixes that you can do. Implement those right away while they're fresh.

5. Make permanent time shifts—updating your Perfect Week, blocking your calendar, keeping notifications off on weekends, and more.

6. Drive the big levers—surely you'll see some opportunities to really scale and take things to the next level. With the renewed energy, improved team and operations, more time, and fresh perspective, lean in! It's a perfect time to catapult to new heights.

That week after is a crucial time to implement. Don't just go back to the way things were. Use the clarity and plan to act on it. It's best to have a good amount of time blocked off for your return knowing that there will be things to create and do.

This will set you up for huge success.

And the thing is… it's not over from here. There's still more to do…

Because the goal isn't to take a 2-Week Vacation by itself. The goal is to create your dream life and business.

So use this time off and the days after to improve your business and time even further, to really set yourself up for ongoing, sustainable freedom.

Again, as I started the book, what you're trying to do is to use this two-week test as a complete break from being stuck "in" the business.

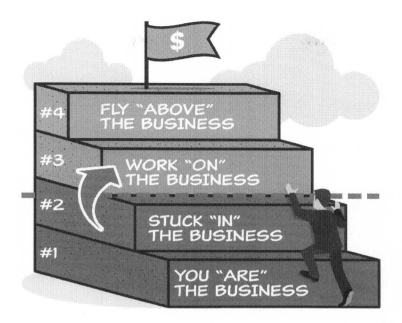

By this point you'll see more of the lifestyle you really want, so let's make that permanent. You'll see more of the business you want—a business you don't need a vacation from. Build the systems and structure to thrive in all ways. Help develop an elite team and set them up to win with more autonomy. And forever improve your business-life integration and balance.

And another important lesson is, know that this is not only a huge opportunity to fix and improve your business, it's a huge opportunity for you as a leader. This isn't a time to bash all of the problems you see. In fact, it's an important time to celebrate! Celebrate your team and all the wins you *did* have.

This is your opportunity as a leader to highlight the positives and what you *did* see go well. Make your team feel really accomplished for handling more, taking ownership, needing you less, making decisions (even if they're not perfect), not being afraid to fail, driving results, and being leaders themselves.

You get more of what you praise!

It's easy to spot the negatives. It's easy to think people don't do things like you would. But the real opportunity is in leaders praising more—and it makes all of the difference.

A popular study featured in Harvard Business Review showed that the best-performing teams have an exponentially higher ratio of praise versus criticism. The low-performing teams had a ratio of nearly three criticisms for every one praise (or a 0.36 praise/criticism ratio). And the high-performing teams had a ratio of 5.6 praises for each criticism![14]

That is a wild contrast (a 15x difference).

RATIO OF PRAISE VS. CRITICISM

TEAM PERFORMANCE

Where do you fall on the spectrum? If you're anything like me, this is an opportunity for you to improve. And there's no better time than after a separated vacation where they step up to increase your praise.

This leads to more engagement and ownership, better team morale, more teamwork, and generally, *more* success. So this is key.

Lastly, let's talk about how to take your renewed energy and keep the momentum going to take your business to the next level. Once you get here, *now* you are in a special spot to be able to really scale and thrive. This isn't the end. It's really only the beginning of what's possible for you now, so congratulations on this huge milestone.

THE POST-VACATION CHECKLIST

1. Complete a full review of the two weeks off (get your team's insights)
2. Create a full list of what to fix or improve
3. Create and improve systems and fix issues (some right away, others create plans to do over the coming weeks and months)
4. Train and develop your team while it's fresh
5. Upgrade your team's responsibilities, giving them more tasks and ownership full time
6. Make the time shifts you identified more permanent, updating your calendar and responsibilities
7. Celebrate your team and the wins you did have
8. Create a Strategic Action Plan—where to go from here (more in the next chapter)

➲ The best way to understand the true health of your business is The 2-Week Vacation Test. With this, one of four outcomes will happen.

- **Stage 1:** Your business would fail pretty quickly without you. You pretty much *are* the business.
- **Stage 2:** Your business would slowly fail and start to fall apart without your direction and work. Your business is still centered around you.
- **Stage 3:** Things would be able to operate fine without you for a few weeks but not grow. Your business isn't reliant on you short term, but it's not advancing much while you're out.
- **Stage 4:** Your business would still thrive and be able to grow without you! This is where you want to be.

➲ Once you get to a Stage 4 business, you join the elite entrepreneurs and have optionality. You can then work as much or as little as you want, scale faster and more easily, sell your business for a high valuation, or work on new projects and opportunities.

➲ The key elements are to make sure your team is prepared before you take time off. Use The Vacation-Prep Checklist as your guide to get your business ready to go so that you can fully disconnect and be confident your team will thrive without you.

➲ Use the time off to refresh and recharge, but also use it as a time to substantially up-level your entire business. By using the Freedom Ramp-Up Process, you'll be improving your operations and team at each step. But even more, once you take time off, you'll see your time and business from a new lens. You'll have ideas for key levers to pull, how to simplify, and much more. So use the fresh perspective to take action and make the changes needed to get you a giant step closer to your vision and Level 10 Life.

- ⮑ On your time off, track: Ideas and improvements you think of, your addictions and mental attachments to the business, the time shifts to make ongoing, and key lessons learned.

- ⮑ Also, have your team keep a log of issues and opportunities while you're out so that they can catch you up on how things went, and get the support they need to improve their role and department with you back.

- ⮑ Then, review the time off with your employees and take quick actions to improve the business, help your team, and give them more ongoing responsibility.

- ⮑ And don't forget to celebrate the wins! Yes, there will be issues and some things that aren't done perfectly, but it's important to praise the positive. This is a key sign of the best teams.

- ⮑ Use this time where you fully separate yourself from the business to stay out of the day-to-day grind. The worst thing you can do is to go back to how things were before you left. Take the actions needed to keep you in a more high-impact role, working "on" the business ongoing and driving strategic growth to the next level.

08

SCALING & LIVING THE DREAM

SCALING TO NEW HEIGHTS

> "The biggest adventure you can take is to live the life of your dreams."
> — **OPRAH WINFREY**

You're close to living the dream.

You have gained back control of your time. You have strong operations, a wonderful team, and a great foundation from which to build. You have a taste of freedom and a much more consistent, predictable business.

But there's one more missing piece that we haven't talked much about. This is the final piece of the 2XOS methodology. And that is to now *scale*!

Now that you have the clarity, time, better operations, team, and the infrastructure to thrive, growth will become exponentially easier, more likely, and more consistent.

Adding some big growth to your time freedom is where you feel *alive*. This is when you and your team feel even more momentum and opportunities are abundant. This is where the fun is, and if you're anything like me, this is an essential part to achieving a truly Level 10 Life.

I'm not going to go into the growth aspects in full detail, as it is beyond the scope of this book. I highly recommend you check out our other 2X resources and programs, as well as my other book, *From 6 To 7 Figures*. But let's touch on a few key points to take into account, especially with the base you've built by following the steps so far.

YOUR BUSINESS (AND GROWTH) IS A FORMULA

Remember, the numbers are the guide. They are arguably your number one tool as CEO and will help be your roadmap to the next level.

By getting free from the weeds, and especially taking time off, you'll have a lot of ideas to implement to upgrade and scale each department individually.

With that clarity, we want to back it up with the numbers by setting new targets for what you plan to achieve.

Let's look at a simple example using the Value Chain.

Let's say that by taking the two-week vacation test and following this process, you get each department to run and operate well without you.

Now you see a couple of levers you can improve for each department to improve.

So, let's say that you see the opportunities and make a clear plan to increase your qualified applications per month from an average of 50 to 75 by focusing on one core channel that is far from optimized. And you make a few tweaks to improve your sales conversions of those applications from 18 percent to 22 percent... And you improve your product and retention, increasing your customer LTV (lifetime value) from $10,000 to $12,000.

What that looks like is this:

	Marketing	**Sales**	**Fulfillment**	**= Revenue**
Metric:	Applications Per Month	Close Ratio (of Applications)	LTV	Sale Value
Current Result:	50	18%	$10,000	$90k/mo.
New Target:	75	22%	$12,000	$198k/mo.

These are all seemingly simple improvements.

But here's the cool thing: The sales from the current result totals $90,000 per month... while the sales total from the new target totals $198,000.

With these numbers, you just more than doubled your sales with small tweaks! And, with this, your costs very likely won't go up much at all—so that means your profits grow exponentially.

Small improvements compounded together on the Value Chain lead to exponential growth!

This is how so many of our private 2X clients have such huge growth. And it's the same for what you can do. So, now that you have more clarity on your business, improvements and opportunities, map out your targets for what you can achieve in the next 90 days and use the numbers as your guide.

DO MORE OF WHAT WORKS

Our "*five-word marketing strategy*" is simple: Do More Of What Works!

It's simple, and incredibly effective.

> # Do this right now: Think of something that is working well in your business. Now, make a simple plan for how you can do *more* of that.

You're welcome. You just earned 1,000x the cost of this book.

It's hard to get something to work well in business. So if you find something that does, do more of it! Scale it.

This is one of the easiest levers to grow, yet many ignore it (without knowing it).

YOUR TIME

The leading indicator of your future success is how you spend your time. (Which is why this book is so important.)

And if you really want to scale, you should be spending at least 60 percent of your time on strategic growth. That's a huge chunk. But you should be able to do that by following the steps laid out in this book.

> **Take back control. Review your time in detail. Get clear on your highest-impact work. Offload everything else. Set the structure with lots of deep work time. And start to get free, one step at a time, to focus on what matters most – in and out of business.**

THE 3-BUCKETS STRATEGY

Growth is great, but you know what's even better? *Consistent, long-term* growth.

The way to get that is by using the 2X Operating System approach and turning your business into a machine. But also with the '3-Buckets Strategy.'

Think of three buckets for your growth:

1. Right Now: the next 30 days
2. Medium-Term: three to six months from now
3. Long-Term: 1+ year out

Do you have a clear strategy and approach for each of the three? So often, we are just focusing on short-term survival (this week or this month). By doing so, we stay trapped on the hamster wheel, constantly hustling for leads and sales.

On the other hand, if you're setting yourself up for long-term success but *not* driving short-term leads and sales, that'll lead to cash-flow issues. You need all three. This is critical.

So are you set up for success and driving actions that will lead to sales and profits in the short, medium, and long term? Every single week, you should be spending a portion of your time on all three. This leads to more consistent and better growth over time.

For instance, this week I've met with our top referral partner to improve that relationship (short term), created and improved an ads funnel for our new lead gen campaign (medium term), and am having some acquisition conversations (long term). All three buckets are filled up.

SHORT-TERM   MEDIUM-TERM   LONG-TERM

> # The reality is, the future arrives faster than you think. Three months goes by in the blink of an eye. And before you know it, two years fly by as well. So you have to start planning ahead and being strategic.

It's the businesses that strategically plan ahead and build for the future (while making sure the short-term is handled) that win big.

While most entrepreneurs are primarily short-term focused, you want to shift to get ahead in the short-term so that you can focus on the medium-term levers. Those are the things that are super important but not that urgent. Those are your *real* moneymakers.

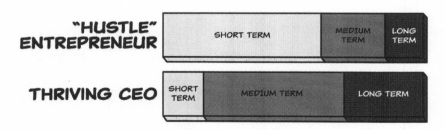

KEEP IT SIMPLE

Now that you have time freedom and things are going well by following this process, don't mess them up!

Many of us entrepreneurs secretly love chaos. When things are calm, we mess them up by trying a bunch more things.

When we have time, we secretly feel a *need* to fill it. We feel like we're not progressing if we're not busy. But doing this process, you have to learn to stop the chaos and keep things simple.

We often want to make things feel more busy, exciting, and like we're *needed* to fix things. We don't consciously know we're doing this. But we do! So be extra careful.

Simple scales. It's a key principle we live by.

Another thing we tell our 2X clients is, "Slow growth is sexy." Yes, our clients consistently grow faster than almost anyone I've seen out there—but it's a result of driving growth in a strategic, simple, and systematic way. Not from trying to do too much.

It's a mindset to build things strategically and systematically over time, not become successful overnight like most try (and fail) to do. Play the long game—and you'll be exponentially more likely to win.

Resist the urge to do more for the sake of doing more. As you get capacity, use the opportunity to *simplify*, not add on more to do. Resist making your business too complex again. Add one strategic lever at a time, and you'll continue to stack brick by brick for an even more successful business.

Done right, you'll consistently grow to the next level and the next level after that beyond your dreams.

RESET YOUR VISION

And the fun part now is that you get to reset. You get to fully redesign your vision and goals.

Once you get to this point, you have a full new perspective of what's possible. You have time freedom, more energy and clarity, and a successful business with momentum.

Now you get to reimagine what's possible for your life and business. It's a whole new world.

So spend some time here. Reflect on what really matters to you. And use this time wisely to fully reset and define your big business goals and complete Level 10 Life vision.

Dream it, design it, and let's go make it happen.

YOUR FIRST 3 STEPS

> "Do not wait until the conditions are perfect to begin.
> Beginning makes the conditions perfect."
> **— ALAN COHEN**

My hope with this book is that you can see that you truly can achieve "it all" in your business.

As I started the book with, the way we see it at 2X, there are three key signs of a wildly successful business:

1. You're **scaling** with consistency and control
2. You're generating **strong profits** and cash flow (and ultimately wealth!)
3. And you have **time freedom**—not being stuck "in" the business, overwhelmed or overworked… so you can live your best life

This is success. This gets you to the point of *optionality* as a business owner, where you get to choose your next best move.

- Do you scale faster and build your empire?
- Do you step back and work less as your business operates?
- Do you exit your business for millions of dollars?
- Do you start new businesses?

Whatever your vision is, when you have more time freedom, profits, and the ability to scale, anything becomes possible for you.

You simply have to follow the proven process to get there.

> **The biggest challenge, however, is you. You will have to change. Your mindset will have to change. You will have to trust more. You will have to let go. You will have to be a new level of leader. You will have to think bigger and more strategically.**

The path is there, but few follow it through.

That's again why the order of growth matters a ton. My goal is to have this book be the playbook for you to follow to live the life you dream about, the reason you started in business to begin with.

My goal is for you to have those memories with your family. To never burn out, ever again. To scale smarter, better, faster and easier. To work less and live more! And to keep the main things in life the main things, not getting sucked into being *owned* by your business.

My goal is to help you unleash like never before. But just know you are going to have to shift in that process. If you follow each milestone, you will change. Your perspective will change.

Don't be afraid of it. Lean into it. Embrace the process. Push your edges. And your wildest dreams will become possible.

I've shared a lot in this book. We've talked about everything from your vision and mindset, to your operations and team, to driving strategic growth. It might feel a little overwhelming from where you're sitting.

So, where do you begin? Here are the three first steps.

SET THE DATE

Do you have your two-week vacation planned and on the calendar? Now is the time to make sure that happens if you haven't already done so.

Let's take this from theory to reality. The first thing is setting the date, then getting some public accountability—family, friends, employees, me. Tell us all. And commit to it.

In fact, put some money down if you can to make sure you make it happen. Buy some flights, or reserve a hotel, or do whatever you have to do to have it be *real* and tangible. Don't just pick a date and do nothing about it. Make it a commitment.

With that deadline set, now it's time to get your business and team ready!

MAP THE ACTION PLAN

How do you eat an elephant? One bite at a time.

How do you create a thriving business machine that can thrive without you? One strategic step at a time.

I've shared a bunch of ideas in this book. It's time to start to map out what you're going to do about it. What are your key actions?

Use the template in your *Vacation Test Toolkit* (2X.co/tools) to get clear on your next two weeks to start to make headway. Things in motion tend to stay in motion, so this is key:

Do. Not. Wait.

Get into motion now while it's fresh in your mind and you're clear on this new vision of growth *and* freedom. Success *and* balance.

The first things I'll guide you through on your Action Plan are:

Simplify—find the areas and things that aren't producing, and cut them out. Simplify. Imagine just overnight freeing up 20–40 percent of your capacity. Reviewing what's not working, and your Low-Impact 80% activities, you can definitely find it. It's scary to cut things out, but life-changing when you do.

Quick Wins: Attack any low-hanging fruit actions. What are some quick wins you can do *this week* to help make for a better business and more free time? I hope you have a lot of ideas from this book.

Time Review: Then, do a deep dive time review. This will help lead to the specific actions to take one by one. The XDS™ process is a great first step here to get clarity.

People Plan: Your team is a crucial part of your freedom and business success. By going through this book, you likely have found some gaps and changes that need to be made there. Create a simple plan for what needs to happen. Who do you need to shift? Who needs to step up or step out? What roles need to be filled? How can you better support them? Get this clear, and you'll see the impact right away.

First Milestones Set: Don't wait to start executing this book. Follow the ramp-up process one by one, beginning with a night and weekend off. Then doing your Done By 10:30AM and Crush-It Day ASAP. The sooner you work through these, the sooner you're ready to start taking your life and business to the next level.

Here's a map (you can download a copy in your *Vacation Test Toolkit* at 2X.co/toolkit) to help you start to map out the dates. Fill this in, and see how quickly you can ramp up. The faster you do, the more that you'll progress—but take it one focused step at a time.

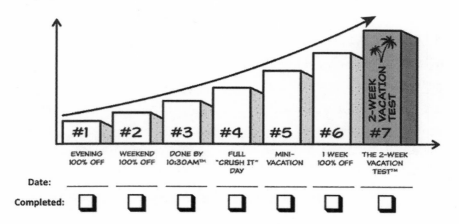

CALENDAR FOR SUCCESS

Time is the constraint to solve for. With the proper time and focus on the *right* actions, you can achieve anything. So let's get that set.

First, simplifying and reviewing your time in detail will help. Then we need to set the structure and calendar for success.

Here's a reminder of what to do for your calendar:

1. Block your personal times (the boundaries of when you'll start and stop work, the non-negotiables, and personal time)
2. Set up your Done By 10:30AM times (at least three per week)
3. Block off at least one Crush-It Day per week
4. Set the meeting rhythm to pulse with your team
5. Batch things where you can and block other deep-work times

And start to create a clear, strategic plan each week. Get this set for yourself and your team. Combine a clear, focused plan with a lot of deep work time, and you're off to the races.

But things related to your time isn't a one-time thing. It will continually shift. So constantly be conscious of where your time and energy are going, and follow these systems on a regular basis.

Remember, how you spend your time is the leading indicator of your future success. With the right actions and focus, it's wild what you can accomplish in the next three to six months.

THE JOURNEY BEGINS

"The journey is the destination."
— RALPH WALDO EMERSON

Years ago, after my first couple of burnout periods as an entrepreneur, I started to make some big shifts. By this point, I was onto my second business that I was more passionate about and building from some of the lessons I learned in my first.

I was on this vacation, kayaking in Alaska with my sister on a beautiful spring day. I was in a narrow kayak built for speed, and long story short, I tipped over in the middle of Glacier Lake—which, per its name, is literally ice water fed by the glacier. There were massive icebergs all around us in the lake, and I was drenched wet, ice cold, trying to balance myself on top of my kayak.

The water was so cold that a few minutes after falling in, my body started shutting down. I was only a few minutes away from hypothermia, and my body shutting down, ultimately drowning in this very deep, very cold lake.

But it wasn't my time. Thankfully some tourists saw me from a distance, and they came to save me.

After surviving and thawing out (which took me hours), I did a lot of reflecting. I went from my life flashing in front of my eyes on the brink of death to getting another chance. It was the perfect time to reflect on what needed to shift.

And the results of doing so surprised me.

You see, I wasn't anywhere near where I wanted to be in life success-wise. I didn't have the massive results yet. But for the first time that I could remember, I'd found something so elusive: true happiness. It wasn't because I had just survived, although that was worth celebrating. It was because I was on my path.

Out of all of the awards, accolades, millions of dollars made, seven-figure businesses, etc., this was the best feeling of success in my life.

I knew who I was, was surrounding myself with great, like-minded people, and was starting to live a life true to myself and enjoy the journey for once. I was on my path...

And I realized that happiness and success are about *progress*.

It's about being on your path, living true to yourself, and embracing the ride on the path to your dream *while* living life in the present.

Reflecting on what I learned, or what I needed to shift after the near-death experience... I realized, not much. I just needed to keep going with the idea that happiness and success are a state of mind, and that true joy and accomplishment are in progress, not a destination you get to. I knew this same mentality would lead to an incredible life.

Maybe, like me, you also have high standards and goals. You don't ever seem *enough* to yourself. You always seem to be chasing.

And as a result, you're spending more time chasing success and being busy than being present—when "success" is right there in front of you. It's a choice, first and foremost.

Writing this book reminded me: **Huge success is hard.**

Entrepreneurship is a crazy stressful thing we signed up for. It's difficult. It's exhausting. But it doesn't make it any easier if we constantly beat ourselves up and stress ourselves out. It doesn't make it any easier if we stay busy on the minutiae, constantly working long hours on mostly the wrong things. Sure, there are issues and fires to deal with. Sure, there is a lot of hard work to do.

But it's about intentionality and working smarter—with the perspective of what you're trying to achieve.

And it's not a destination.

Start living your life *now*. You don't have to wait until your 2-week vacation to start living.

You don't have to wait until you're a multi-millionaire to be happy.

You don't have to wait until your business is a full machine before you start enjoying the process and being a better leader.

You don't have to wait for... anything.

If you enjoy the journey on the way to that next level of success... you'll be happy when you get there. If you don't, guess what? That next level won't fix things.

Success amplifies. It doesn't fix.

So I want to wrap up this book with this lesson:

Live your dream life starting right *now*. Enjoy the process *now*. Embrace the ups and downs and lean in *now*. It all starts with a mindset shift.

Get clear on a worthy destination to work toward, surround yourself with people you enjoy, and embrace the journey. Lean in. That's when you really win—and get on your path.

So don't delay. Start your journey to freedom today and let this be a turning point.

The time is *now*.

With that:

> Get clear on a compelling vision of your dream life and business…
>
> Create a simple and focused strategy to make that a reality…
>
> Build and optimize your operations and team as you get free, taking it one strategic step at a time…
>
> And create a wildly successful business as you live your Level 10 Life.

It's all within reach.

To your success,
Austin

DREAM IT.
DESIGN IT.
DO IT.

THE VACATION TEST TOOLKIT

"Ideas are worthless. Execution is everything."

— **MARK CUBAN**

To achieve big success, it's not about ideas or information. It's about implementation and execution.

This book would be a waste if you don't put it into action. So to help, I've put together a list of the top resources I've mentioned in this book to help you implement these strategies and systems right away.

This is valued at $497, but it's 100% FREE as part of this book. It's all in one central place for you here: **www.2X.co/tools**

Inside, you'll find a host of resources you can use to get free and grow a much healthier business and team, including:

- Swipes
- Proven systems
- Specific templates
- Example spreadsheets
- Custom PDF worksheets to fill in
- Deep-dive training videos
- And more.

This is 100% FREE to access directly here:

>> 2X.CO/TOOLS <<

THE 2X ACCELERATOR

The way we see it at 2X is, there are three key signs of a wildly successful business:

1. You're **scaling** with consistency and control
2. You're generating **strong profits** and cash flow (and ultimately wealth!)
3. And you have **time freedom**—you are not stuck "in" the business, overwhelmed or overworked… So you can live your Level 10 Life.

It's easy to get one of these three from your business. It's pretty easy to get two. But it's extremely hard to get all three.

Well, we work hands-on with ambitious six- and seven-figure online and service-based entrepreneurs to help you implement the proven systems and strategies we've optimized for years so you can achieve all three.

We take a holistic approach to business growth, guiding you step-by-step to optimize your strategy, free up time, improve your team and operations, and drive consistent, predictable growth and profits. This way, you go from "stuck"—working "in" the business and not growing like you know is possible—to scaling with consistency and control.

In just a few years, we've helped businesses generate over $255 million and counting while in our 2X coaching programs and have helped free up countless hours of time.

To get the hands-on support to free up time and scale a wildly success-ful business, visit:

2X.CO/2X

More Time | Bigger Profits | Faster Growth

ABOUT AUSTIN NETZLEY

Austin Netzley is a business investor, advisor, author, and entrepreneur.

He is the Founder and CEO of **2X** (2X.co), a business coaching company helping 6- and 7-figure entrepreneurs scale exponentially through operational excellence.

In just a few short years, Austin and 2X have helped private clients generate over $255 Million in revenue by implementing the proven 2X systems and strategies.

2X has been highlighted as one of the Inc. 5000 fastest-growing companies in back-to-back years, as well as featured on many of the world's largest business outlets, such as *Forbes, Entrepreneur, Yahoo!,* ABC, NBC, and more.

Austin is a former collegiate athlete and engineer before becoming an entrepreneur starting various businesses. He is the best-selling author of several books, including ***From 6 To 7 Figures***: *The Proven Playbook To Get More Traction, Free Up 20 Hours Per Week, And Scale Past $1M In Revenue!*

For more information about Austin and 2X, please visit: 2X.co

ONE FINAL REQUEST

"In a gentle way, you can shake the world."
— **MAHATMA GANDHI**

If you got value out of this book, would you do me a favor?

Would you please share this book with ONE entrepreneur friend or peer who needs this?

I've found the strategies and process in this book to be life-changing, and I've seen it so many times with our private clients. So I want to help more entrepreneurs…

- Take back control of their time
- Build a much healthier, more successful business
- And start living their dream life (in and out of business)!

Can you help me change the world one entrepreneur at a time, and share this book with someone who comes to mind?

It's my belief that entrepreneurs are the leaders of our communities and society. Together, we can free up countless hours from the minutiae of business and build incredibly more success.

So, please share this book and let's make a difference together. Your support means a lot.

>> 2X.CO/VACATION <<

Made in the USA
Coppell, TX
12 August 2023

20265743R00141